"Aurora Lassaletta writes an insightful and engaging account of the consequences of her brain injury which is truly inspiring. This book succinctly describes and demonstrates with such clarity the invisible consequences of traumatic brain injury (TBI) that so many experience but find it tricky to explain. Throughout the book she takes us on a journey through these consequences and how she comes to learn to work with them to lessen their impact on her day-to-day life. Her honesty and openness about the ongoing process of acceptance and reflections on identity within this context is so important in gaining insight into the psychological challenges faced following a TBI. This book will be of great value to those who have experienced a brain injury and their families as well as to clinicians and researchers working in the field. I would encourage everyone to read this book who has experience of or interest in the impact of acquired brain injury. Thank you for sharing your experiences."

– **Fiona Ashworth**, DClinPsych, AFBPsS, Anglia Ruskin University, UK

"Wow! This book captures the essence of the brain injury experience brilliantly. It is written in clear language that is easy to read and digest, addressing all the common challenges that people with brain injuries and their families go through in a way that few other such books have done. As both a clinical psychologist and a brain injury survivor, Aurora Lassaletta uniquely applies insightfulness and keen observation to her personal journey from 'normal life' to injury and on through years of rehabilitation and personal growth. Her message of perseverance and hard work and hope is an inspiration not only for survivors and their families, but also for professionals, who will undoubtedly re-think their stereotypes of rehabilitation as mostly impairment-based and only relevant in the acute stages of injury. I can't wait to have the book in hand to recommend to my colleagues and clients with brain injuries alike."

– **Jill Winegardner**, PhD, Director of Neuropsychological Rehabilitation, University Hospitals Cleveland Medical Center, Cleveland, Ohio, USA

"This book, written by a colleague, provides a moving, honest and brave account of the experience of suffering a traumatic brain injury. The narrative and commentary vividly brings to the reader the sheer determination, professional support, and resilience required to make the long journey back to living a meaningful life after suffering a traumatic brain injury. It is essential reading for all of those interested in the real story of what long-term rehabilitation after traumatic brain injury actually entails for many people."

– **Rudi Coetzer**, DClinPsy, School of Psychology, Bangor University, UK

The Invisible Brain Injury

The Invisible Brain Injury recounts, in her own words, the experience of Aurora Lassaletta, a clinical psychologist who suffered a traumatic brain injury (TBI) after a traffic accident. Presenting her unique dual perspective as both a patient and a clinician, Aurora highlights the less visible cognitive, emotional and behavioural symptoms common to acquired brain injury (ABI).

This moving account showcases Aurora's growing awareness of her impairments, their manifestation in daily life, how they are perceived, or not, by others and the tools that helped her survive. Each chapter combines Aurora's perspective with the scientific view of a professional neuropsychologist or physiatrist who provide commentaries on her various symptoms.

This book is valuable reading for professionals involved in neurorehabilitation and clinical neuropsychology and for clinical psychology students. It is a must read for ABI survivors, those around them and clinicians, who are all an essential part of the rehabilitation, adjustment and acceptance process involved with ABI.

Aurora Lassaletta had to stop her work as a psychotherapist in a public mental health service in 2005 due to her TBI. She undertook a path of learning and improvement that she still follows today. At her new pace, Aurora enjoys helping other survivors learn to live with ABI through psychological support groups.

After Brain Injury: Survivor Stories

This new series of books is aimed at those who have suffered a brain injury, and their families and carers. Each book focuses on a different condition, such as face blindness, amnesia and neglect, or diagnosis, such as encephalitis and locked-in syndrome, resulting from brain injury. Readers will learn about life before the brain injury, the early days of diagnosis, the effects of the brain injury, the process of rehabilitation, and life now. Alongside this personal perspective, professional commentary is also provided by a specialist in neuropsychological rehabilitation, making the books relevant for professionals working in rehabilitation such as psychologists, speech and language therapists, occupational therapists, social workers and rehabilitation doctors. They will also appeal to clinical psychology trainees and undergraduate and graduate students in neuropsychology, rehabilitation science, and related courses who value the case study approach.

With this series, we also hope to help expand awareness of brain injury and its consequences. The World Health Organisation has recently acknowledged the need to raise the profile of mental health issues (with the WHO Mental Health Action Plan 2013–20) and we believe there needs to be a similar focus on psychological, neurological and behavioural issues caused by brain disorder, and a deeper understanding of the importance of rehabilitation support. Giving a voice to these survivors of brain injury is a step in the right direction.

Series Editor: Barbara A. Wilson

Published titles:

Rebuilding Life after Brain Injury
Dreamtalk
Sheena McDonald, Allan Little, Gail Robinson

Family Experience of Brain Injury
Surviving, Coping, Adjusting
Jo Clark-Wilson and Mark Holloway

The Invisible Brain Injury
Cognitive Impairments in Traumatic Brain Injury, Stroke and other Acquired Brain Pathologies
Aurora Lassaletta

For more information about this series, please visit: https://www.routledge.com/After-Brain-Injury-Survivor-Stories/book-series/ABI

The Invisible Brain Injury

Cognitive Impairments in Traumatic Brain Injury, Stroke and other Acquired Brain Pathologies

Aurora Lassaletta

Translated by Ruth Clarke

Routledge
Taylor & Francis Group
LONDON AND NEW YORK

First published 2020
by Routledge
2 Park Square, Milton Park, Abingdon, Oxon OX14 4RN

and by Routledge
52 Vanderbilt Avenue, New York, NY 10017

Routledge is an imprint of the Taylor & Francis Group, an informa business

British Library Cataloguing-in-Publication Data
A catalogue record for this book is available from the British Library

Library of Congress Cataloging-in-Publication Data
A catalog record has been requested for this book

ISBN: 978-0-367-25404-9 (hbk)
ISBN: 978-0-367-25407-0 (pbk)
ISBN: 978-0-429-28762-6 (ebk)

Typeset in Times New Roman
by Swales & Willis Ltd, Exeter, Devon, UK

To Nacho, Álvaro and Mateo,
thank you for your daily support. I love you.
To my parents, Aurora and Luis, and to
my brothers Luis and Álvaro,
thank you for inspiring me with the motivation to
face challenges.

Contents

Contributors

Amor Bize López. Neuropsychologist. Centro Estatal de Atención al Daño Cerebral (CEADAC). [State Centre for Acquired Brain Injury Rehabilitation in Madrid]. Systemic family and couples therapist.

Susana Pajares García. Physiatrist. Centro Estatal de Atención al Daño Cerebral (CEADAC). [State Centre for Acquired Brain Injury Rehabilitation in Madrid].

Christian Salas Riquelme, PhD. Clinical Neuropsychologist. Clinical Psychologist. Clinical Neuropsychology Unit, Cognitive and Social Neuroscience Laboratory (Facultad de Psicología, Universidad Diego Portales). Santiago, Chile.

About the author

Figure 0.1 Photograph by Sergio Parra

Aurora Lassaletta graduated in Psychology at the University of Comillas, Madrid, in 1995. She specialised in Clinical Psychology (PsyD) in 2000, after a 3-year Psychology Residency Program at Hospital Universitario de Guadalajara in a rotary training period, with internships in different mental health services.

During these years she was also trained as a University Specialist in Individual and Group Psychotherapy, as well as in Gestalt therapy.

She developed her professional practice as a clinical psychologist in different mental health services, working as the Coordinator of the

Children's Unit at the Montreal Psychiatric Day-Hospital in Madrid and as a Psychotherapist in the Spanish NHS in her last years of practice.

In 2005 she suffered a traumatic brain injury (TBI) as a result of a serious road traffic accident that stopped her professional career. This encouraged her to undertake a path of learning and improvement that she still follows today.

Since 2009 she has collaborated with acquired brain injury (ABI) associations and rehabilitation centres on a regular basis, contributing her experience as a patient and as a psychologist. Aurora has created very useful strategies during her acceptance process, and she has learned to embrace her new identity and to focus on what she can now handle. At her new pace, Aurora mostly enjoys helping other survivors learn to live with brain injury through psychological support groups. She is passionate about increasing awareness around cognitive, behavioural and emotional impairments.

Contact: www.danocerebralinvisible.com

Note

This book incorporates two points of view: that of Aurora, and that of the neurorehabilitation clinicians Amor Bize, Susana Pajares and Christian Salas. To distinguish the clinicians' paragraphs from the main text, these will appear in italics.

Preface

From the very first time I met Aurora at CEADAC (State Centre for Treating Acquired Brain Injury in Madrid), in April 2007, I was impressed by her ability to describe the practical repercussions of the effects we had long been studying in theoretical models for cognitive function. When she decided to put all these vital experiences down on paper, I knew that the result could be something very useful for patients and relatives as well as for clinics that are in contact with people who have suffered brain injury.

My part in this process was simple: as an additional rehabilitation session, once Aurora had compiled all the information relating to her life after the accident, we organised the chapters according to cognitive, behavioural, emotional and physical symptoms, to structure the text. Within the cognitive symptomatology, we classified them according to the main functions that were altered: attention, executive function, memory, etc. In each section we incorporated annotations "from the specialist's point of view" in the explanations for what Aurora was describing, to give more meaning and weight to each of the impairments discussed.

Personally, I think Aurora has captured a vivid picture of everyday life with the most common cognitive changes following a brain injury, and has done so in a fun and entertaining way, despite the serious personal repercussions of many of the situations portrayed.

As a neuropsychologist, it makes me very proud to see a former patient write a book. All the more so if it will shed some light on changes that, in the vast majority of cases, go unnoticed and are hard for professionals, families and even patients themselves to understand. However, this is a clear example of resilience, the ability we have to overcome difficult situations and emerge from them somehow stronger. Aurora shows us this every day.

I would like to thank Aurora for being brave enough to take on this project and for her trust in inviting me to collaborate with her. I have learned just as much as she has from the process. I encourage readers to investigate the finer points of brain injury through these pages – I am sure they will fascinate and inspire.

Amor Bize López, neuropsychologist at CEADAC

Part 1

The invisible brain injury

Chapter 1

The invisible brain injury

Aurora Lassaletta

Introduction

In May 2005, as the result of a serious traffic accident, I suffered a significant head trauma, along with multiple fractures. At the time, I was 33 years old, married, a mother of two – my eldest child was two and a half, and the youngest just five months old – and I worked as a clinical psychologist in a public mental health service.

I had the immense good fortune to be in the hands of some incredible doctors, thanks to whom I am now able to write this book. Following emergency neurosurgery to resolve the most immediate consequences of my cranial fractures, and two weeks in an induced coma, I spent a long time in hospital. There followed weeks of rest, and many months of physiotherapy and physical rehabilitation, which were slow but effective, and gradually, with time and effort, I was able to move into a wheelchair, and from there to walking with crutches, and little by little, without them.

I noticed that the people around me linked my physical improvements to an overall improvement. Yet, day-to-day, I was noticing new impairments, which I attributed to the accident, that did not only affect mobility. It was hard for me to understand why I was so tired all the time, despite being inactive; why couldn't I follow long conversations or large group discussions? Why couldn't I read or understand a film, when I had all the time in the world? Why was I speaking slowly and less able to retain information? And worst of all, why couldn't I stand the normal noise of my children playing nearby?

With my restless and inquisitive nature, and my former training as a clinical psychologist, I tried to understand and analyse the new impairments I was observing. This constant study of my own symptoms was a vital tool in learning to live with them.

Since I looked normal, and hadn't suffered serious language impairment, many of the cognitive difficulties that I was mentioning to people were not easily identifiable from the outside. Perhaps I wasn't able to explain them very well. Many people confused my apathy, slowness, difficulty concentrating, inexpressiveness and some of the other side effects that I describe in this book with symptoms of depression.

Some of the professionals, when they heard about my cognitive impairments, referred me to the Centro Estatal de Atención al Daño Cerebral Adquirido (CEADAC), the Spanish State Rehabilitation Centre for Acquired Brain Injury in Madrid, for a neuropsychological assessment. The fact that I didn't have very visible injuries led to a few mix ups, such as the visit to the health centre's social worker who had to fill in a referral form for me and asked, "Why didn't Aurora come?", since she was expecting the person referred to in the report to have more visible injuries. I can really empathise with Sophie, who suffered a brain injury as a result of encephalitis, when she describes in her account how, because she shows no residual physical disabilities, people don't understand that she feels fragile, tired and confused on the inside (Easton, 2016).

At CEADAC I received short but excellent treatment, focused largely on attention and organisation, thanks to which my family and I could begin to understand that there was a reason for many of the cognitive impairments I had been noticing. Until then we had been living with these impairments on a daily basis, but we didn't understand them, and we didn't know how to manage them, because we didn't know that they were caused by a traumatic brain injury (TBI).

Magnetic resonance images (MRI) later showed my neurological damage for the first time: extensive left frontotemporal injury and diffuse axonal damage. I was very surprised to hear the doctors who saw the results say, "Poor thing, you must be exhausted!" That had been my main complaint for the last few years, and nobody was listening. It took nearly two years for me to be diagnosed and to receive suitable rehabilitation for my impairments and proof from neuroimaging that showed the damage. I wouldn't want this to happen to anyone else, but, from what I have heard in my groups and what I have read over the last year, it is actually quite common. I really identified with Karen, in the interesting book *Life after Brain Injury: Survivor Stories*, who was also treated for physical fractures after her accident, but took six years to get a diagnosis of TBI (Wilson, Winegardner and Ashworth, 2014).

After the MRI results, I was lucky enough to meet a doctor and psychotherapist with extensive knowledge of the brain and its disorders. Her first goal, before she started any kind of psychotherapy work with me, was to identify which symptoms were organic and which were emotional. I am very grateful to her; she was the first person to start teaching me the differences and to propose the right treatments. At first, I also believed that all my symptoms were psychological. It is certainly normal to have some, given how difficult it is to adapt to such a sudden change, and they could even aggravate some of the symptoms of brain injury. Now, knowing how to tell the difference and knowing which symptoms are related to the injury, I can be kinder to myself, and I think that sharing my experience could help other people in similar situations to feel better. I have undoubtedly gone the long way round sometimes, but I have learned a lot along the way.

My aim in writing this book is to show some of the symptoms of acquired brain injury (ABI), especially in the cognitive area, which I consider to be the most invisible from the outside. I would also like to reduce the added frustration involved in dealing with these symptoms throughout the process toward recovery without knowing that they are the result of a brain injury. I think it is important to try to raise knowledge and understanding of these deficits in people who have suffered an ABI, because one very common symptom is a lack of awareness of what is happening to us. The book is primarily intended for people affected by brain injury and those around them who are an essential part of the rehabilitation, adjustment and acceptance process, as well as professionals in contact with this group. I would also recommend it to lawyers and insurance brokers who have to determine the damages and necessary rehabilitation for each client. It is very important that we all know that there are residual effects that are not immediately apparent but are just as disabling and require long-term rehabilitation.

My journey to this point has been hard work – both physical and psychological – especially the continuous task of accepting the extent of the effects imposed by each impairment at every moment. I believe that this constant acceptance is fundamental, for both the person affected and the people around them.

My normal appearance meant that I spent a lot of time in the first few years justifying myself and explaining my impairments whenever I was unable to perform a task, since outsiders often expect me to have the speed, agility and normal coping mechanisms that I appear to have. We're not inventing our symptoms! But we're often treated as though we're exaggerating them (Wilson, Winegardner and Ashworth, 2014). As Jade Roberts points out in the book *6 Steps to Understanding and Coping with Mild Traumatic Brain Injury*, it is practically impossible to maintain the right pattern of cognitive and emotional deficits to fake a brain injury (Roberts, 2014) – so, please, believe us and listen to us!

Now I find it much easier to live with, knowing that there is some neurological damage, especially cognitive effects, that can't be seen from the outside, and I no longer feel such a need to explain myself. From what I have seen, it is much easier to tell that someone has brain injury if they have a significant physical impairment. I laugh whenever I recall the day that I feigned a limp and managed to go straight into the swimming pool with the Brain Injury Sports Club, sick of always having to stop and face the same question when whoever was on the door didn't recognise me as a member of the club: "And where do you think you're going?"

The majority of my physical injuries were reversible, due to the areas of the brain affected and thanks to the rehabilitation work. Those that remain, which limit me every day, are not so visible from the outside. These days, if you don't know my story and you're not with me for twenty-four hours straight to witness the changes during the day, I'm sure you wouldn't be able to tell that I had significant physical or cognitive impairments. Some brain injury is only revealed by living with the person, not in a half-an-hour medical appointment.

I have noticed significant improvements in my cognitive symptoms over the twelve-plus years that I have spent rehabilitating in one way or another. I have been able to recover most of the English that I spoke, my typing, my coordination in swimming and my reading, without working on any of those things specifically, but from neurorehabilitation work overall. I am lucky enough to be able to talk about some of my problems in the past tense, and to have reduced the extent of some of my impairments, after many years of hard work, research and inquiry. Functional MRIs have shown that some impaired functions in the affected cerebral hemisphere have been transferred to the healthy hemisphere. I found confirmation of these results in the investigations presented by N. Doidge in his book *The Brain that Changes Itself*, which reflect the incredible neuroplasticity of the brain (Doidge, 2007). These results give me strength and the hope that I can carry on recovering skills even now, and encourage others to keep trying. I know that the path to rehabilitation and rediscovering your "place" in the world is hard, that it takes determination and patience and that, despite all the outside help and being surrounded by people who love us, we often feel extremely alone, which can lead to depressive thoughts, as described by many survivors (Yeoh, 2018).

It's not that the injury is invisible because it is slight. My own injury, although I believed it was slight, was more than that, and the professionals are still reminding me of that today. Why doesn't it seem disabling enough to be unable to go back to work or to organise your own house?

For a time I felt like the accident had robbed me of my identity as a woman, mother, partner and professional, and I felt like I had to invent a new one. Now I realise that I am recovering some of the features of my old identity and I can integrate them into the new one. What I hope is that I will accept and be at peace with my new reality. My dream is to get the most out of life, to give as much as possible of myself and feel useful as a person and as a professional. I know I'm going to get there.

After many years and a significant improvement, as a family we are managing to adjust and accept our new roles more. I am very pleased that my son Álvaro, the eldest, likes to cook, and he can help to organise and prepare the lunch or dinner if I am very tired. On the other hand, my youngest son Mateo has some kind of sensor that detects when I need peace and quiet, and makes sure I get it.

With my current work on acceptance I feel that I'm making progress when I manage to connect to myself, to know where I am, to be realistic about my plans and to not deny my impairments. I can do this by putting into practice the mountain of resources and tricks that I've learned along the way. I want to share all this to see whether my experience can help other people in my situation.

The history of the book

In this book, I will try to explain the physical, cognitive and emotional changes that I have noticed since the accident, and especially the ones I have been writing in a very disorganised diary over the years.

I've always needed to write down my experiences. I still have all my diaries from my childhood and adolescence, and, as an adult, I still jot down my thoughts and feelings on paper, in notebooks and even in notes on my mobile phone, although I never read them again. Now, several years after the accident, with encouragement from the professionals working with me on my neuropsychological rehabilitation, I have decided to collate many of the notes I've written over the last few years about the impairments that appeared and the treatments and tools I used to alleviate them, and turn them into a book. These professionals told me that my diaries showed my dual perspective: as someone affected by brain injury and as a professional myself.

When I shared my plan with friends with editorial experience, they suggested that I should organise what I was writing with a contents list, and I decided to separate what I had to say about each impairment, which became the different chapters. The observation and follow-up of these symptoms over the years has been an incredible learning experience, in terms of their nature, management and development. I only had a basic concept of neuropsychology, which I learned during my training as a psychologist, but, fortunately, I still have some of my professional skills for observation, analysis and investigation. These have helped me to explore the symptoms in detail, despite my current internal disorganisation.

I asked myself many times whether the symptoms I was writing about were already part of my personality before the TBI, and I still wonder whether these physical, cognitive and emotional changes are just a natural development for my age or the result of not being in work – although I could tell that they were clearly related to the brain injury. I decided to get it confirmed and show my writing to an expert on the subject, Amor Bize, a neuropsychologist at CEADAC, who was responsible for my treatment there in 2007. I remember that, when she discharged me, she was the first person to encourage me to write. She said that I explained very clearly what happens to people with ABI. At that time I couldn't set myself a task like that, as I couldn't even stay focused long enough to read a novel. I was buoyed by her enthusiasm, telling me that my intuition and observations were correct and that the symptoms of brain injury I was writing about had been clearly identified.

Another help with confirming my observations and continuing to learn was my experience in the ABI psychological support groups, which I coordinated on several occasions as a voluntary psychologist at CEADAC. At those workshops, I met survivors of TBI, stroke and different ABIs who had no outwardly visible injuries. And others who had more physical injuries, but shared many of the same symptoms that were imperceptible from the outside. Being able to talk about how difficult this could be at times was very beneficial for everyone.

Something that always came up in those groups was the relief that we all felt when we realised that some impairments we had, which sometimes we had not identified as the effects of brain injury, could be given a name. It is also very important that the people around us recognise these impairments and realise that there is a reason for them. And the most important thing of all: not feeling bad for having them. This really helps in the difficult task of acceptance.

For the majority of symptoms, I tried to follow an outline that reflected the following points:

1 "How do I recognise it?" Description of the symptom and how it manifests in daily life.
2 "How has the symptom been changing and developing over time?" Treatments, differences.
3 "How do I feel, and how do I feel that others perceive it?"
4 "What do I do with this?" Resources and strategies for compensating.
5 "What do the experts say?"

At first, with minimal understanding of my deficit, I had planned to do the last part myself and started my research in neuroscience books to understand and learn about every symptom, as if I were the person I used to be. After an initial period of frustration, I realised that these days my ability to learn is slow and I carried on focusing on the experience part. I decided to ask the neuropsychologist Amor Bize to collaborate with me and to provide a scientific review, as a specialist, of the symptoms I had identified.

The fact that we worked together was crucial for me in the process of creating and organising the book. She helped me to order and structure my account of the symptoms that I showed her, and to shape the book. She wrote paragraphs to be interspersed throughout mine, presented here in italics, explaining in the more technical language of her own specialism the cerebral changes corresponding to the different symptoms explained in my personal accounts.

It was a very stimulating and rehabilitative task because we had to set ourselves deadlines, which helped me to plan, although it also made me face up to the impairments I was talking about and keep considering them in every situation, discovering and learning things about each symptom as I observed it and time went by.

I tried to plan the book with consideration for other affected people who would read it and their attentional difficulties. This meant that I tried to write easy-to-read paragraphs that are not too long. I also asked the professionals who collaborated in the book to write their coloured notes with accessible words.

The contribution of the physiatrist Susana Pajares, also from CEADAC, was very helpful when explaining the physical side of the symptoms, as was the input from Christian Salas, clinical neuropsychologist and psychotherapist, in discussing the emotional aspect of identity reconstruction.

There are many books that offer lengthy descriptions of the symptoms of ABI. In 2007, when I finished my short treatment at CEADAC, I looked for books that would help me to understand what was happening to me, and in Spanish I only found technical books, with language that was too difficult to understand. These books didn't mention the problems a person with ABI faces in everyday life; they didn't describe the subjective experience of living with residual disabilities that are invisible. I found no books written by other survivors in my own language. That would also later influence my motivation to publish what I had written.

In this book, I collate, in the form of experience-based accounts, the symptoms that I know best, because they have affected me most intensely and because I have seen many of them replicated in various people in the groups I coordinated. Of course, some of the symptoms are worse in me, and some in others, depending on which hemisphere or area of the brain is injured, or whether the damage affects a broader or more specific area. Over twelve years of contact with people with brain injury, I have been able to see how each ABI is unique, even when they share the same areas of damage (Wilson, Dhamapurkar and Rose, 2016). In addition to the injury, the person's previous personality and *cognitive reserve*, meaning their previous level of intellect and education, also influence the effects (Stern, 2007).

When I set out to write this book, I stopped reading others on the same topic. At that time, at the height of my insecurity, I wanted my book to show who I was, without being influenced by anything I had read. Now, I have gone back to looking for books and thirteen years after the accident I've been able to start reading in English, which has been significant progress for me. In this language, I did find books by other people affected by ABI and by professionals who explain many of the things that I talk about. That was a big surprise. For me, it was also important to read work by other psychotherapists and healthcare professionals affected by ABI, and to learn about how they are coping with their residual disabilities now. If only I could have read those books during my first years of rehabilitation! They would really have helped with understanding, recovery and hope in the acceptance process. I decided to incorporate these new references into my original book to add knowledge and testimonies, and to make sure people know about them. I have also recently found works published in Spanish that help to raise the visibility of ABI.

Writing the book has been a vital experience and an intense learning process. I especially want to thank Amor Bize for her collaboration, hard work and constant support over the years, which meant that the project could go ahead. And, above all, for treating me as an equal. Also Susana

Pajares for contributing a medical viewpoint. Thanks, too, to Álvaro Bilbao, author of the prologue for the Spanish version of the book, for dedicating his time and incredible vision. Thanks to Christian Salas, who I met at his workshop on emotion after ABI, when I made my first return to a conference after thirteen years, and from whom I am still learning. I will never forget the generosity, friendship and incredible work of these professionals. I would also like to thank Barbara Wilson for believing in my book and letting me share my experience in her series.

I will always be deeply grateful to all my family, friends and the professionals and countless people who, over all these years, have been by my side, helping me to get better and make this book a reality. I cannot fail to mention, with heartfelt thanks, the two strangers who unknowingly made this challenge possible: the two doctors who, in May 2005, stopped to rescue me at km 100 of the N-VI motorway between La Coruña and Madrid, just outside Sanchidrián, and took the necessary clinical measures to ensure that I was quickly in the hands of a neurosurgeon who, together with his team, saved my life at the Hospital Universitario de Salamanca. They were my anonymous "guardian angels". I hope that one day I will able to meet them again and thank them in person.

Part 2

Cognitive symptoms

Chapter 2

Cognitive symptoms related to attention

Aurora Lassaletta and Amor Bize

Neurological fatigue: continuous energy calculations

"Neurological fatigue" – as I call it, to differentiate it from normal physical, mental and emotional fatigue – has been with me from the outset. It is still there, although less severely after my neuropsychological rehabilitation and learning to manage it with the tools I have acquired. I have consulted many medical and psychological professionals, from neurologists and psychotherapists to nutritionists. When this fatigue hits, it blocks my (now limited) mental ability, because I have less energy, which needs to be distributed carefully. This fatigue calls for the body and mind to relax, or even sleep.

> *Whenever brain injury occurs, there is some extent of neuronal death, and if we imagine the brain as a computer, this translates to a loss of resources for processing information. Our computer now has less memory to execute programs that we used to start running automatically. In fact, now we might need to shut down one program before opening another, because we can't run multiple programs at once. This is why people who have suffered a brain injury take longer to do things, get tired more quickly and get overwhelmed if they have to do several things at once.*

I would describe neurological fatigue as a weight that I carry around with me, which at some times is more intense than at others. I am learning to live with it. Once I start any activity, physical or cognitive, it will appear after a short time. It doesn't always settle in immediately – sometimes it takes a while to manifest itself physically. This is why it is important for me to prevent fatigue, because, if I ignore it and prolong the activity that is causing it, it becomes accumulated fatigue, which is much more severe and difficult to overcome in a short space of time.

> *A very common effect following brain injury is that, because the resources for processing information are now more limited, they are not managed as effectively. Multiple activities cannot be performed because the "manager" of these resources has not been able to estimate what is required to reach a particular target, or has allocated lots of resources to one phase of the process, leaving insufficient resources for other phases. In this way, the person feels that they cannot take on everything; they get tired quickly and have to rest after being active for a while (Sohlberg and Mateer, 1989).*

When I came out of hospital, even though I was on complete bedrest, the fatigue was significant. I needed to sleep fifteen, sixteen, even seventeen hours per day. Everything was exhausting: talking, listening, thinking. At first, I attributed this tiredness to my physical weakness. But as time went on and my body became stronger, I realised that, even though this fatigue was worse if my body was unfit, being unfit was not the cause. It was something deeper and more difficult to explain.

After the accident, mental fatigue would appear after approximately twenty minutes of a normal level of attention and comprehension – at that time that was too much work for my neurones! As Cheryle Sullivan, a family doctor with ABI, says in her book, when fatigue set in it was so intense that her only option was to stop what she was doing immediately. It was as though all the lights had gone out. She also talks about the different tools she learned to use to cope with it (Sullivan, 2008).

Afterwards, I got much better; now I can stand up to an hour and a half of activity that requires a lot of concentration, a little longer if it's a light activity. If I listen to a talk, read a book, watch a film, attend a course or make any intense cognitive effort, once that time has passed, the mental exhaustion starts to appear, along with the feeling that I don't have the resources to face it. This even happens in deep conversations, after which I feel like I have switched off because of the exhaustion. This mental fatigue then combines with and increases physical fatigue.

> *With the spontaneous development of the brain following a brain injury, and even more so with rehabilitation, the management of these processing resources gradually improves. Although we don't have any more resources, the "boss", who decides what to allocate where, is more efficient, and manages to complete more tasks with*

less fatigue. Tasks that are performed more often can also become automatic over time, which means we don't have to do them consciously but on "autopilot", which requires less attention.

My first neuropsychological assessments in private centres, before I came to CEADAC and before my brain scan, always lasted a maximum of one hour. I remember one appointment when someone congratulated me on my results and told me that they were very good, some of them were even above average for my age group, and that really I had no significant neurological damage. They explained that, with exercises, I would recover the functions that had become rusty through disuse. To me, these comments – which I repeatedly heard from specialists over many years – made me happy, but they also worried me, because I was playing down my fatigue and sometimes even criticising myself for feeling that way, given how well they said I was doing. When I left the office where I had my assessment, walking to the hospital exit, I had to sit down in the waiting room. The fatigue from making a moderate cognitive effort had set in: it was mental and physical and it stopped me from moving on to the next activity. It took me half an hour to get my mobile phone out of my bag and call my family to come and get me. My husband, Nacho, used to say, half joking: "If people don't know you, you can fake it for an hour, an hour and a half, but that's it".

It is important that neuropsychological assessment and rehabilitation allow the saturation of processing resources and fatigue to appear, and that behavioural observations are made. On the other hand, essential information is provided by the individual and family interview about how a typical day goes, how many hours' sleep are required (this always increases following brain injury), how many naps and for how long, what type of activities that the person used to enjoy have they stopped doing (family meals, shopping centre visits, etc.)

I will never forget arriving at CEADAC to start treatment. I could tell that they really had a deep understanding of brain injury. First of all, my assessment took a whole day, because they told me that it was important for them to see my progress through the day, and they could see how my performance weakened significantly and my fatigue increased the longer I spent on a particular task. Similarly, they told me that my rehabilitation treatment, for the same reason, should be at least four hours per day. They had a room where I could go to sleep for a while if I found one of the therapies exhausting. It was wonderful to allow myself to be tired, to feel tired and to have a neurological explanation for it. I remember having to use that room quite a lot at the beginning, and little less at the end. Above all I remember how much calmer I felt knowing that it was available. I learned a lot there, and I could see that the team of professionals treating me understood exactly what was happening to me, and I could breathe and relax so that I could get the most out of my months of rehabilitation.

The four hours of treatment at CEADAC were too intense for me, and caused considerable fatigue. Afterwards I had the feeling that I had reached my limit, as though I had no energy left, physically or mentally. My physical therapy at the centre was incidental, because in my case, at that time, the priority was cognitive rehabilitation.

During treatment, the professionals mentioned that I seemed like a different person depending on the time of day: early on I had more mental agility, and after a few activities I was exhausted and slow, and I had difficulty understanding what they were telling me.

Many people – including some professionals, before they did my brain scan – had told me over the years that my fatigue was completely normal for someone my age with small children. I disagreed. I think the most tiring time with the children was months before the accident, going back to work after maternity leave with my second child, when I wasn't sleeping much because the little one was still having midnight feeds and the older one woke up more and was acting like a baby again. Of course I was tired then, but even in that situation I could still keep up enough strength to do my intense job. I remember, at that time and with lots of enthusiasm, starting to run a group for adolescents at the mental health centre, a task that also took up a lot of energy. However, with neurological fatigue, you often can't even find the motivation.

The million dollar question for people with ABI is, "But why am I so tired?" I have always asked doctors about this fatigue and they tell me that it is very common, but nobody has explained, even in simple terms, what really causes it. Each time I understand a little better that it is not simple and that it has many contributing factors.

In the support groups I have sometimes run at CEADAC, with ABI survivors, the issue of fatigue always emerges as one of the most significant impairments we have to accept. I remember how much I identified with one of the participants when he said, "I feel awful for feeling tired, when I'm not even doing anything! And when my family asks me to help around the house and I tell them I can't because I'm exhausted, they get annoyed, and I get angry with myself, too". Knowing that intense fatigue is very common for people with brain injury was a relief for him, and helped him to be kinder to himself. He was attributing his fatigue to a lack of motivation, labelling himself "idle" and criticising himself for that.

Personally, I was thrilled whenever doctors in different fields suggested doing a particular test on me that could give an explanation for my fatigue or other effects: "I think you must have terrible anaemia", "Let's give you a hormone injection to see how your adrenal gland reacts, and I'm sure that will give us an explanation". They thought that my symptoms would be reflected in the test results. Normally all the tests came out fine, which I was very happy about, but I would sincerely have liked to have a biochemical explanation for some of my impairments, to seek possible treatment. It also cannot be explained as an emotional thing, an easy conclusion to jump to when tests are shown to be within the normal range. "I'M NOT SAD, I'M TIRED!" has been my cry on many occasions. Because I know perfectly well what it feels like to be sad; I've had moments where my mood was really very low. My family and I, now, with time, can tell the difference between the apathy and tiredness of depression and the fatigue of brain injury.

This means that, for me, day-to-day life, working at the same pace as everyone else – the pace of social or school life – is really exhausting. I almost always manage it, but it takes a lot of energy. When I am left alone and can choose what to do, I avoid stimuli that I find exhausting.

The first time I went to a specially adapted swimming lesson at the sports centre, for which I had to submit a medical report, I explained to the teacher that I had to start slowly and build up the effort gradually. She, seeing that I had no significant external physical effects and looked normal, would keep telling me, "You can do much more, come on, come on, don't be lazy!" I found it very hard not to try to meet her expectations, but I felt ill and decided to leave the class early. I got out and started to feel sick and dizzy, and had to see the sports centre's doctor, who told me that my symptoms were due to overexertion.

I learned from this and now, in the sporting activities I do, I ask for half the time, in both paddle tennis and swimming. I only do sporting activities led by people who specialise in sport with brain injury, and I try to stop physical activity when I feel like I have reached my limit, whether people understand this from the outside or not.

The work of accepting exhaustion is fundamental. In my daily life, I have kept coming up against this limitation and crashing straight into it in all kinds of situations. Now I really take it into consideration, although sometimes I do tend to play it down, and even ignore it. Nacho helps me a lot; he recognises it and anticipates it, sometimes even before I do.

I know that good planning, not doing activities that are too much for me and learning to stop when I need to are indispensable resources. Fortunately, I have stopped thinking that exhaustion will just disappear the next day, or, like when I was young, with a couple of cans of Coke and a quick nap in an armchair.

I am beginning to understand, from what certain professionals have told me, that there are other variables that also influence fatigue, including sensory impairments, such as my hearing and sight loss. For me, it is exhausting trying to pay attention to, and even more so trying to understand, all the visual and auditory information I receive, when it is already more difficult for me to see and hear.

In reality, I realise that now, after living with this fatigue for over fourteen years, and having got much better, I have become an economist. I spend the day calculating energy consumption. I plan my movements, my comings and goings, my travel: wherever I go, in the metro or the car, I'm always taking into account how much energy I will use and how much I will have left.

As I have come to accept this impairment, I am more able to predict which things I will be able to tolerate, physically and cognitively, and which I will have to do without. People may think that a metro journey with one change is child's play, but for me, from the perspective of fatigue, it is not. It's not just about physical fatigue; for example, the noise of the metro really bothers me. I have to add that fatigue to the next thing I want to do. It is true that I am more tired in the afternoon and at night, because this fatigue has been accumulating.

Now, for example, having spent an hour and a half revising this chapter, I feel like I have exceeded my mental capacity, and I have a headache and serious mental exhaustion. Whether I like it or not, I will have to stop for quite a while and rest.

I am eternally grateful to my friends for giving me a "taxi voucher" to go to CEADAC and back. At first, I went there and back on the metro, with one change and a ten-minute walk to the centre; that way, between the treatment and the journeys, I ran out of energy. In the afternoon I did not feel strong enough to go down to the park with my children, or take charge of everyday activities. My friends understood and supported me.

When I or someone else suggests an activity that I know will tire me out physically or cognitively, I have to find a time for it in the morning, when I will be more rested. The workshops and groups that I run have to be first thing in the morning, and last a maximum of one hour. I still need to sleep after lunch – luckily, I'm reducing the length of those naps as time goes by, with continued rehabilitation and recovery, but if I skip it, it will usually take its toll. As noted by G. Denton, being more or less aware of our own energy levels explains how we treat ourselves and how we treat others. Being more aware helps us to plan the right tools to handle fatigue as well as possible (Denton, 2008).

I wish I had known from the beginning that tiredness was such a frequent and common symptom for many people with ABI, whose experiences I can now read in English (Winson, Wilson and Bateman, 2017). I would have been kinder to myself. I also believe it is vital to include the treatment and management of fatigue in neurorehabilitation from the start (Wilson, Winegardner and Ashworth, 2014).

Attention difficulties

Problems with attention and divided attention are difficulties that my whole family has been aware of from the very beginning. When I came home from hospital, it was summer and, along with Nacho and the children, I moved into my parents' house in the mountains. Since I had to get physical rest, my family and friends tried to be around, visiting me and keeping me company all the time. I also got a lot of phone calls, and this whole situation made me very anxious without really knowing why. Gradually, I realised that I wasn't able to follow a conversation when there were more than two people in the room or there was background noise.

> *Attention functions are transverse cognitive functions, which means that the performance of other cognitive functions depends on them. In reality, without attention we can't perform any voluntary activity, which means that, where there is a brain injury, we see changes in attention. Attention is a very complex cognitive function that encompasses everything from staying awake to focusing on things that interest us, maintaining concentration and even being able to divide our attention between various tasks. Following a brain injury, we can find all or some of these components affected to varying degrees (Benedet, 2002).*

My parents left newspapers and magazines out for me; my eldest son and my niece would come in from time to time to tell me things; they brought my little son, who was just a baby, for me to play with. And for me, focusing on any of these tiny things required so much effort that I would often disconnect and not focus on any of them, or I would fall asleep immediately because the situation was exhausting for me.

In the book *Survivor Stories*, Robert, who was affected by ABI following a stroke, recalls how his new hypersensitivity to background noise meant that – as happens to me – he couldn't pay attention to anything when there were two or more people in a room (Wilson, Winegarder and Ashworth, 2014).

> *Following brain injury, people prefer calm situations that do not deviate from their routine and do not involve being bombarded by visual and/or auditory stimuli. This is because their resources for paying attention to what is happening are limited (neuronal death has occurred) and their capacity for separating what is important from what is not important has been altered, meaning that they are inclined to pay attention to everything. Furthermore, people who have suffered brain injury are unable to focus their attention on one thing, so everything that happens attracts their attention and they lose track of what they were following, which means they can't keep up with a conversation between several people, for example (Bilbao and Díaz, 2008).*

They also gave me lots of books, films and music, and whenever I settled down to enjoy one of those things, I realised it was impossible to concentrate on it.

> *The ability to maintain attention for a period of time also tends to be affected after brain injury, which means that people need a frequent change of activity.*

In the two years following the accident, when I tried to read something that interested me, I lost concentration after a short time, without knowing what I had read after a few minutes. I realised that I could only sustain my attention for a short time. Later I would manage to read a chapter of a novel in snatches, but I needed to underline the main ideas and afterwards I would not remember what I had read. I was only able to read, bit by bit, one very short news article each day, the kind that you usually get in free newspapers. I would get my family to bring a copy home from the metro, because I liked those articles for their simplicity. I still do.

It took me over three years to read a short, easy novel, and I could only do it if I had total peace and quiet, free from the interference of noise and other stimuli. Comprehension and attention are very closely related. Fortunately, I can now read for a long time without any problems, and even though I have got a little better at isolating myself from background noise, the best way I find to concentrate on a book is to read at night, in bed, when the children are already asleep.

I can't remember things if I haven't paid close attention. In the first two years, I couldn't keep my attention on a series or film on the television. If they started talking very quickly, I couldn't follow. I noticed that my mental functioning was much slower than before. After these two years I did manage to watch one film at the cinema, *The Illusionist*, but after a while I lost the thread because I couldn't sustain my attention. I needed Nacho to explain it to me and remind me of the plot when we left. The other film, which I watched on DVD, was *Habana Blues*, which I had seen four years earlier and enjoyed very much. I found it difficult to follow and there were many things I couldn't remember; to make matters worse, the protagonists spoke very quickly and in Cuban slang, which I used to understand, but not now.

Ten years after the accident, I successfully managed to keep up with two television miniseries at the same time, with interest and anticipation, sustaining my attention and motivation all the way through each episode. Before, I would intend to do it, but not succeed. It is true that, while I try to follow them live, if I don't feel like I have the attention span on the day the programme is broadcast, I can make use of technological advances and multimedia, record them and watch them at a quiet moment.

In many of my sporting activities, I still get distracted easily and, especially when I have to pay attention to several things at once, it drives me crazy! Doing Pilates, suddenly I have to watch my breathing, tilt my pelvis and lift my leg. I feel blocked: either I do one thing or the other. The same happens when I'm playing paddle tennis: I have to pay attention to several factors and I can only focus on one. Lately I can relax and try to focus on just one of them, and I have realised that if I'm calm I am more able to give my attention to more than one thing. Christopher Yeoh explains that during his treatment he was fortunate enough to take some neurology classes where he learned that distractibility was one of the most important symptoms following a brain injury. During his rehabilitation sessions, he had to learn to control it in the various tasks he was set, where his difficulty concentrating on one thing became clear (Yeoh, 2018).

> *Divided attention is one of the cognitive abilities that people with brain injury miss the most, even many years after it happens, as this is a highly complex faculty that requires the efficient management of processing resources, dividing these resources rationally to be able to do everything (which is often impossible). Some authors prefer to*

talk about alternating attention, which is the ability to switch your focus back and forth between tasks; for example, when driving, I pay attention to the pedals, shift to the traffic lights, then to the gear stick (Sohlberg and Mateer, 1989).

I belong to a choir, and that is where I notice the biggest improvement when it comes to attention: not getting distracted by the score, the melody, the breathing, the pitch. When they ask us to do body percussion at the same time as singing, I find it complicated. I have to know what I'm singing by heart, and be able to do it automatically so that I can dedicate space in my brain to moving my body. Rehearsals are late, and often I can't go because I'm too tired or because I'm going through a difficult time with my physical problems, but I do love my choir! Music has made me feel happy in myself again. Even though I can't remember the words to the songs very well, even though I get too distracted in rehearsals and then I struggle to find time to study at home, the music and my experience in this choir take me to a very special place within myself.

With rehabilitation and training in day-to-day activities, certain simpler or more repetitive processes can become automatic, so that they take up fewer processing resources (they are not consciously performed) and that means these extra resources are available for new activities (for example, body percussion when I already know the words to the song).

Listening to the doctors, initially I could only pay attention to the first thing they told me, and then I switched off. I think the problem with attention is very closely linked to my lack of energy and how quickly I feel my brain is saturated. It's as if I stop paying attention in preparation for the saturation or overload that is coming.

The cognitive system "self-protects" against saturation, and when that happens, we "switch off". This can be easily observed in babies or small children, who fall asleep in particularly noisy situations, like a party with loud music, because they can't carry on processing such powerful information any longer.

I find dividing my attention very difficult. My female friends joked that I was turning into "a bit of a man", based on the stereotype that men are incapable of doing two things at once. Before, I was quite used to doing several things at the same time, and improvising solutions to whatever came up. Now, in my new situation, I have to make sure things are finished before I start any more.

While I have been able to resume some of my normal daily activities my attention problems manifest themselves most of all in a high level of distraction. I find it difficult to differentiate the essential from the secondary, and therefore I waste a lot of energy thinking about or paying attention to unnecessary things.

> *Paying attention to a situation overall is a very complex faculty that requires a lot of processing resources (attention, reasoning, memory, etc.), which is why people who have suffered brain injury usually focus on one aspect and do not assess how this aspect is essential overall. For this reason, they are often found to require help or supervision with important life decisions, although not with everyday ones.*

It is very hard for me to focus my attention on the present, on what I have to do in this moment. I remember that, at the Brain Injury Rehabilitation Centre, my therapy involved sitting at a table with people solving crossword puzzles and other manual activities, while others talked and listened to the radio in the background. I couldn't stand it and asked them to let me move to a quiet corner of the room, where I could do my rehabilitation better. That was when they explained that the important thing for me was to keep paying attention in that context. Luckily, I've been improving a lot and, now, even when I find myself in situations where I cannot pay attention, or find it very difficult to do so, because I already know what will happen, it isn't as stressful. Mindfulness, a meditative practice that focuses on "the here and now", also helps me in these situations to come back to myself, to sustain my attention or, if that is not possible, simply to be calmer.

It makes me laugh to remember how I rejected the sudokus that they asked me to solve in CEADAC. I told them that they were a fad and that years ago we had never heard of them and we got along just fine without them. At first I couldn't do them, and the concentration, inability and frustration exhausted me.

> *In neuropsychological rehabilitation, it is very important to explain to patients why we suggest each of the activities, because it is normal (and natural) for them to question the need for many of the activities if they don't see a practical application in their daily life. This is why we should explain which cognitive processes are engaged in*

these tasks and how they influence those processes on a daily basis (Wilson, Evans, Gracey and Bateman, 2009).

I remember how nervous I was a few years ago doing the interviews for someone to help me with some of the household chores. At that time, if my children were around, playing or talking, I wasn't able to listen to what I was being told by the interviewee and I couldn't understand what was happening to me. I got very angry with my children and didn't know how to fix the situation. Now, this happens much less, and I am aware of it, so I send my children to another room, or if I need to do an interview like that, I do it at a quiet moment, while they are at school.

When I'm tired I know that my reflexes and attention are at their worst. It has taken me several years to start driving again, until the professionals saw that I was ready, and I know that I can only drive if I am relaxed and my mind is clear. I am always very strict about this, but even more so when I have my children or anyone else in the car. It used to be impossible for me to drive with music playing, but now I can do it on simple journeys. If there is any other intense interference, like two people talking loudly beside me, or a more complicated route, I automatically turn off the music. I often ask for silence in the car, when I feel like I need to focus my attention on something more important.

Even though it looks bad if I'm with people who don't know me, I will often leave before the end of an event, or a class, because I figure that, if I make it to the end, I will be too tired to drive. In this regard, my priorities are very clear, and I never take the car if I know that an activity will be long or intense.

Starting to drive again is a very important milestone for many people following brain injury. However, driving does not just mean handling a vehicle; it is an extremely complex activity that takes place in communal space, where the driver's actions have clear consequences for other drivers and pedestrians on the road. There are many cognitive functions at work when we take the wheel: attention, reaction speed, shape recognition, decision-making, etc. This is why it is so important not to start driving again too soon or without having gone through the necessary procedures and assessments to do so safely.

My attention still lapses, and the latest incident had unfortunate financial consequences. I use an app on my mobile to park in regulated parking service areas. When I registered my car on the mobile app, I wasn't paying much attention, and I entered the letters of my car's registration plate before the numbers, instead of the other way around. I started getting fines, as if I hadn't paid, but the money was being deducted from the balance on the app. I even received emails confirming my parking and my payment. Not even by appealing the fines could I get out of them. Until one day, in desperation – after I found yet another fine on the car, even though I had paid – I asked one of the parking service agents for help. He very kindly spent a while investigating what was happening with my phone, until he found my mistake. It didn't help me get back the money I had angrily spent on fines, but it did save me a lot of future expense.

To cook, I need a lot of peace and quiet. Since this is not very common in a family kitchen, and I can't give 100 per cent of my attention to just one thing, the result is that I burn myself quite a lot, so lately I will always ask for silence before I move anything hot, and my family are starting to understand.

Often, the people around me don't understand that interference prevents me from paying attention properly. The other day, we were taking a long car journey – I never drive in those cases – and took a relative with us. The children were listening to music and the relative was talking to me. I asked my children to turn the music down, and they did, and I still wasn't able to pay attention to what the person was telling me. I told her about my difficulty, and asked if we could continue the conversation when we reached our destination. When she kept on talking and telling me things, I decided to switch off, and I could do it without worrying. When we reached our destination, I was able to confess that I hadn't been listening to the last twenty minutes of the story, and she would have to repeat it.

At my children's old school, the kids put on some great musicals and many families go to watch them at the weekend. There are usually very small children in the audience, and during the shows they will frequently talk, cry and laugh. If there is this kind of interference, I can't pay attention to what is happening on stage and that used to make me very anxious. At first I would demand silence and launch furious glares at the main offenders. Now, knowing that this is due to my own difficulty, I try to take my place early and sit at the front. If I can't do that, I get annoyed by not being able to hear, but knowing why means I can handle it better.

At group meetings with the teachers from school, courses and conferences, I have had to change the way I usually do things. I always used to sit near the back of the room or venue; now I sit myself in the front row so I can focus my attention and avoid constant distractions.

The more conscious I am of this difficulty, the more resources I can use. I remember a dinner where my brother-in-law used his mobile phone to play me a song written by my nephew, so that I could listen to the lyrics. There were a thousand different background noises and other conversations, and I wasn't able to make out the words. When I realised, I told my brother-in-law that I couldn't hear it that way, but could he please start it from the beginning again and pass me the phone so I could put it to my ear. That way I had no problem focusing my attention on the beautifully sensitive lyrics.

Not long ago, I heard some news about the difference between reading paper books and electronic books. I have read some things in electronic format, but I prefer to keep reading on paper – that way I can tell how far I am from the end, judge my progress or go back to previous pages if I need to refresh any information. Curiously, I had a feeling, as I told Nacho, that with electronic books I forgot things more easily. And the news just confirmed that it is easier to retain information you read in traditional books than in electronic books.

> *Reading a physical book does give many contextual cues that an electronic book lacks (book size, cover image or colour, number of pages read or to read) which help us to recall the content of what we have read.*

Just one intense thing a day! The saturated hard drive

The best image to explain what happens to me mentally when I receive too much information, whether auditory, visual or emotional, is a saturated hard drive. It's as though my information folder is smaller now and gets full almost immediately. When there are too many visual or auditory stimuli, I get bewildered, and blocked.

I have often thought that the feeling of being less able to learn or retain information might have something to do with my age, with the fact that I don't have a regular working day where my neurones are functioning continuously. But I can tell that this is also a consequence of the TBI. If I look back, I can see that, being a restless, curious person, and very keen to recover, in all these years, there hasn't been a single month when I didn't do rehabilitation or stimulation activities for my brain, so I have no doubt that it has been continually working. In reality my aim for many years, which I can now see was quite unrealistic, was to be able to go back to my job as a clinical psychologist, which I loved. I felt that to do that I had to engage and recover all the functions I had lost, by doing varied and continuous work and rehabilitation.

The other day, a friend told me the story of a relative who had just left the ICU after a stroke. His family were very angry with him because he would close his eyes every time the window was opened or visitors arrived, and he only wanted his children to go in. I could really identify with him, and I advised her to respect his process. I explained that, at this point, noise, light and other stimuli would certainly overload his brain and that he would not be able do everything. I suggested that it would be better, in the beginning, to have visits from people he is very close to, one-to-one, and for them to respect his rhythm and need for rest and peace and quiet, because I understood that the slightest thing could overwhelm him. I have a slightly guilty memory of how I would cut short visits, even from people who had travelled a long way, or simply refuse to see them, at times when I was overwhelmed and couldn't deal with any new stimuli.

> *The capacity to process information following a brain injury is often significantly limited, and while we are gradually able improve this capacity, the individual's rhythm should be respected, limiting the quantity, variety and duration of stimuli (Wilson, 1999).*

When I got back to walking, for a long time I would meet up with a friend who had taken a year off work. Our children were at school together, and we always tried to meet up at the park or plan something together. She always preferred to be outside, as did I, years ago. Yet, in this period, I needed the opposite: I would prefer to invite people to my house, to be on "my territory". Now, I realise that I needed quiet, familiar surroundings, without too many new stimuli, to make sure I didn't get too tired and my hard drive didn't get saturated. If I was in the park or doing any new, noisy activity for too long, I noticed that it was as though something had shut down, as though I stopped understanding, and I couldn't even follow the conversation with my friend anymore.

> *It's good for people with brain injury to stick to routines in familiar surroundings where they can predict what is going to happen and what resources they have. This way, they can dedicate attention to other tasks, and don't need to improvise their performance while they're on the go. Improvising is highly demanding for our brain! (Bilbao and Díaz, 2008)*

After many years, I was able to start attending a few one-off courses, interesting conferences or events, and enjoy them. It is true that when auditory or visual information is intense or difficult, I can only pay attention and understand for a limited time; after that, I get saturated.

A while ago, I decide to attend some systemic psychology workshops that lasted three hours each. At the first one, I had to leave half way through, because I could tell I had reached complete mental saturation, and at the exit I had to get some air and sit still for a while on a bench before I could make it to the bus stop to go home. I have got much better, and two years later, in the latest workshops, I can make it through the whole session, although I do the mental trick of disconnecting when I can see I'm reaching my limit. When I have no way to get away from the noise, or the auditory, cognitive or emotional stimulation that is saturating me, I have learned to do a quick mindfulness exercise that really helps me to tolerate the situation, and to relax, focusing my attention on my breathing instead of on the stressful stimulus. Thanks to this technique, which I use like a game, I can reconnect to the activity after resting my brain for a while. Although I miss a bit of information by using this tool, I can continue with the workshop, and I've made a few wonderful friends who will give me their notes if I need them.

When it comes to auditory information, I have noticed that there are a lot of variables at play. I get saturated immediately if there is sound coming from different sources at the same time, because I have problems with divided attention. Auditory interference seriously hinders my information processing. I understand that, at the moment, it would be impossible for me to work in a shared, open space.

I remember my first trip to a shopping centre, close to my in-laws' house – Nacho went with me, holding my arm – so that I could choose the showerhead to put in the bathroom that we had been forced to refurbish. It was a very specific trip, on foot, very quick and easy. But with the street noise, the number of people we had to dodge, the shopping centre lights and the exhaustion, I remember it like a huge expedition to Everest, which left my body exhausted and my mind saturated for at least a week. My "hard drive" still wasn't prepared for a trip like that.

An impairment with processing information from visual or auditory stimuli is closely related to a person's emotional burden, and mine increases when this burden is greater or particularly affects me.

The other day, my parents invited me to a wonderful performance at the concert hall, and just before I went in, a friend called to give me the news that her husband had lost his job unexpectedly. That news affected me and the emotion did not leave me the mental space to deal with anything auditory or visual. My right eye, due to an injury to one of the cranial nerves in the TBI, does not have complete mobility or open fully. When I'm tired or saturated, it moves and opens less. Shortly after the beginning of the show, my eye wanted to look away and close. The saturation prevented me from enjoying the concert.

My mother suggests tonnes of plans and activities that she knows I enjoy, such as classical music concerts, ballet, shows, operas. I think she's gradually coming to understand why I turn them down more often than not. Even so, I'm lucky to have her making suggestions, and I hope that one day I'll be able to enjoy them. I need to have had a very quiet day and been able to take a nap to be able to go out and enjoy an event like that. If there have been other activities during the day, even everyday things, I feel like my head is saturated and I can't take in anything new, even if the plan sounds very appealing. If I've had an active day, and I also have to prepare dinner and ask one of my children questions to prepare for a test they have the following day, my hard drive will almost "crash" and I can't add any more files.

> *Some people with brain injury need to cancel any activity outside of the house during the entire day if they plan to go out in the evening. This way they can be sure to reach the end of the plan having enjoyed it. Knowing what resources we have prevents us from taking on more responsibilities than we can handle.*

A while ago, my school friends, who I see once every six months, met for tapas at the Mercado de San Miguel. I was very excited about seeing them and visiting the new market. It seemed like a fun and unusual plan. That morning I had had a neurological check up at the hospital and I had spent an hour talking about my current condition and summarising the most obvious progress and effects, and listening to the doctor's opinions and recommendations. For me, something like that is an intense event, with lots of stimuli – including the journey – and an intense event is something that will saturate my brain. Afterwards, I took a nap, but my head was still exhausted. I had the feeling that I couldn't handle any new input. In that case, new input could mean listening to stories from my friends, or visiting the market, or simply leaving the house. All that, plus a metro journey with one change, seemed completely impossible, and I called to say I couldn't make it.

I came up with the motto of "JUST ONE INTENSE THING PER DAY!" and I always try to stick to it. I was able to fully enjoy the last dinner a friend organised at her house, with some dear friends from out of town who were passing through Madrid. I considered the night a success on my part, thanks to good planning and preventing overload by asking my parents to look after the children that day after school so that I could get a proper rest before dinner.

One day, the Spanish Federation for Acquired Brain Injury (FEDACE) invited me to give a talk as a mother, a psychologist and a survivor. I told them my motto and they liked it. Giving that talk was intense enough for me, but in the afternoon I had the funeral of someone close to me, and I wanted to be with the family from the start. However, the motto proved true, and I fell asleep after the talk, unconsciously turned off the alarm and arrived at the funeral late and angry with myself.

It's incredible that I seem to be becoming more like children or old people, in that they need routine and things to be repeated. I don't think that this is down to a personality trait in me, as much as the fact that routine and repetition, at the moment, mean that my brain doesn't get tired, that it doesn't need to use up more energy than usual to adapt to new stimuli and doesn't get saturated too quickly.

My desire to know more about what is happening to me makes me more observant. One day, I heard someone in my paddle tennis class say that she has good vision in both eyes, but she doesn't register what she sees on the left. That fact stayed in my mind and I recalled it as I sat down to a family meal and realised that for the last few years I had been quickly choosing the same seat. The same thing happened the next day when I was looking for a place to sit in my mindfulness workshop: I realised that I always look for a place on the same side of the room and I need to see the teacher from the same side. Suddenly, it all started to add up and I understood that, although to a lesser extent, it is also much easier for me to process information that comes from the right. It also happens at conferences and concerts, and when one of my children comes to show or tell me something. This discovery is making everyday and social situations much easier.

> *Hemineglect is the difficulty in registering stimuli that appear in one visual field, usually the left. It can also affect other sensory modalities, such as hearing or touch. People who display hemineglect have no physical changes (loss of vision, for example) to explain it, yet they are unable to pay attention to what is happening on that side. As such, in its most severe form, they might ask for bread at mealtime when it is already on the table but on their affected side, or apply make-up to only one half of their face (Benedet, 2002).*

I have come to the conclusion that I can't go anywhere where there are too many people: parties, crowds, demonstrations or the Rastro, Madrid's flea market, at busy times. In these situations, there are too many stimuli for me, and they are all happening at once: auditory, visual, cognitive and emotional. It's an overload for my brain. When I have, on occasion, ignored that rule and gone anyway, I felt bad and afterwards my body, and especially my brain, really let me know. I needed to be in "flat mode" for a couple of days.

> *People with brain injury often avoid family dinners, weekend trips to shopping centres and, in general, any situation that means they will be bombarded by visual and/or auditory stimuli. The capacity we have to differentiate important information from unimportant information, and to allocate processing resources only to the former, is often lost, which means that people "have to" pay attention to each and every one of the stimuli they receive, and this is why the processing system collapses in these situations. It is common for these people to become more irritable, and to get angry when they don't have the necessary resources to escape that environment.*

My most recent experience of overall physical and mental exhaustion was on a trip to Italy with the family, a trip that I had helped to organise at my own pace and in my quiet moments, looking for cheap flights and accommodation. In Rome, at the Vatican Museums, we had a fantastic guide but, after a while of trying to listen and understand the information she was giving us, I felt that my cognitive capacity was completely saturated, that I couldn't take in any more information. I didn't acknowledge it, because I didn't want to miss anything, I wanted to keep listening and learning. After an hour and a quarter walking around different works, stopping a while in front of each one, listening to the corresponding explanations, I felt like I couldn't take any more, not just mentally, but physically, too. I had to go back to the apartment and blank out for a couple of hours. Although I lay down to rest, I didn't sleep; it wasn't so much a physical tiredness as a general saturation. I needed to have no stimuli for a long time, because my brain couldn't process anything else, I needed silence, to be alone. I couldn't even bear the sound of anyone else resting next to me. I don't know how well the people around me understand that, but it is very important that I spot it and can remedy it when it happens. Luckily, my family support me and respect my rest. We have learned a lot from living with the consequences of exhaustion on many occasions.

> *When saturation of resources occurs, people can become "void" or "disconnected" until they rest and recover their spent resources. Behavioural changes can also appear, such as irritability and clear signs of frustration (irritation, raising the voice, kicking or punching walls). This is why it is so important not to put people in situations that exceed their capacities and to increase these demands gradually (Goldstein and Beers, 1998).*

For me, it is essential to have realistic expectations of what I can do now. When I spend an hour running the support group afterwards I'm quite exhausted and saturated, but very happy. If I talk about the group from a distance or think about it in theory, it seems simple. They have even asked me to volunteer to run more groups per week but, after years of living with my injuries, I am aware that my capacity is limited, and that it is essential to acknowledge and accept those circumstances, which is why I knew I had to say no. It was sad, but it was realistic.

Brain sluggishness: orders take time to arrive

A few years ago, after the accident, when everything in my brain was still happening very slowly and some of its connections – now more recovered – were not working, there were some tense situations in my family when Mateo, my youngest son, was crying in his crib and I didn't go to him immediately. I got angry with myself and so did people around me. It wasn't until sometime later that we all understood that, even though I wanted to stand up, the order from my brain to my legs didn't arrive for quite a while, which is why, even though the idea of standing up was there, the movement started much later.

When I listen to myself speak, I usually can't tell how slow I am but, from the outside, seeing myself on a video or asking people who know me, I realise that this slowness is noticeable. I recall the honesty of a psychotherapist, asked to make an assessment when she met me, at a time when I thought I was pretty sharp and clear-headed. "I didn't know you before", she said, "but you can definitely tell that you're slow to express yourself". Although that was difficult to hear, I appreciated her frankness. Knowing that the way I experience things is different to how other people perceive them is very important as I continue learning. My children also tell me that I talk slowly, especially when I'm tired. In her book *One Long Journey*, written following her experience of suffering a stroke, the Spanish actress Silvia Abascal makes similar reflections on this new slowness and needing more time to develop a thought in your mind before expressing what you want to say (Abascal, 2013).

Brain sluggishness manifests itself particularly in reaction times, and sometimes being aware of these slow times makes me frustrated – it can provoke either apathy or explosive outbursts. Faced with different stimuli, my hard drive becomes saturated, and I jump around impulsively, or I freeze, taking even longer to make decisions because I'm blocked.

Three years ago, once I had regained my English, I decided to join a course below my previous level, and I realised that I have a problem with my mental speed. Before, I was very quick, but now I can't keep up with the fast pace of the class. It's like my engine is running on fewer revolutions. In class, we were asked to do exercises in groups of three, and everyone else would have the answer before I had even finished reading the question.

In listening exercises, when we were listening to news headlines on English radio, projected from a website, I had to close my eyes, because I couldn't pay attention to the visuals, the sound and the distractions around me at the same time. In these circumstances, I think that the ideal would be for them to play it to me in slow motion, because all of a sudden everything seems too fast.

When we were given a text, I could identify and recognise the English words, but sometimes I couldn't remember the word in Spanish, even though I knew the meaning. Sometimes the teacher would ask me something I knew the answer to, but I took a long time to give it, or I went round the houses. I get anxious when I notice this, because it's as if the idea comes at one speed, and the expression comes much more slowly. I also realise that I often struggle to express myself articulately.

To use smartphone games as an example, a good reflection of what happens to me is that I'm good at Words with Friends (I can play at my own speed, I have plenty of time, I can work without pressure, and there is no single correct answer, there are thousands of possibilities and I can do it my own way), but I am awful at Trivial Pursuits (it's about remembering information, and I'm terrible at that, and there is a limited time and only one correct answer, with no room for creativity).

Before the accident, I was a good skier, and I really enjoyed going to the mountains. Many people ask me why I don't start skiing again; I could start with my children, albeit at beginner's level. But now, the orders from my brain don't reach my legs in the same way, I don't feel like I have full control over them, which makes me afraid to do anything that isn't automatic. And skiing is anything but automatic. You have to watch out for uneven surfaces, ice, and of course the slope. That would be too many things to consider at once, and the excessive attention and lack of automatic action would not allow me to ski or enjoy myself.

> *Following brain injury, processes that used to be automatic and required very few cognitive resources now need to be performed consciously, and therefore it stops being so easy to do them at the same time as other activities. For example, people who are being trained to walk again have to stop walking in order to respond if someone asks them a question. Gradually, they become able to maintain a conversation without stopping walking, and even to solve complex mathematical problems during a rehabilitation session.*

Mental sluggishness increases considerably with tiredness. I perform much better if I can go at my own pace, if I don't have any interference that makes me feel stressed and when there is no pressure of time. For example, last summer's beach holiday was a very relaxed week for me because we did not share a house and we were able to set our own schedule. Although it took longer to do things, and sometimes we were late eating meals or going down to the beach, it was a real break not to have rigid schedules.

I have realised that I put a lot of energy into normalising my symptoms. I try not to give the impression of having injuries or disabilities. If I relax and let out what is really inside, I talk much more slowly and move at a slower pace. This makes me think of what I call the "Friday rest". On Fridays, I force my pace, like I do every morning, to get my children to school on time, with all the effort that involves, and then I go to the pool with the ABI Sports Club. Despite my laziness, and the physical effort and fatigue that that little bit of exercise will mean, the best thing about that moment is being able to be myself, to go at my own pace, and being surrounded by people who know what's happening to me and don't expect anything more than what I can give at any particular moment.

I am very happy to know that I have physically recovered to the point that I can play a short game of paddle tennis with this club, when I am feeling physically well. And it is fun to see what happens in the game. When I think I'm sure to hit the ball with the racquet, I usually miss; I get there a second too late, because my movements are slower, and I would say my reflexes are, too. But, being aware of this delay, I have learned to try to hit the ball before I should. When I remember to use this trick, I'm sure to hit it! The speed of paddle tennis also frightens me, for example when the ball comes at me suddenly. Now, it's amusing to see how I choose my opponents in games according to how aggressive or competitive I think they are. I need to be up against someone who plays at my speed.

Something similar happens in choir. Lately I have been trying to increase the speed of my singing to keep up with everyone else's tempo.

Plans go more slowly than I first think. I often come up with a plan of action and then see that I have calculated the timings wrong, overestimating my own speed. The frustration helps me to get my act together and, even if things happen later than they were supposed to, they still happen!

A few years ago, my eldest son, Álvaro, surprised me with a comment about my mental speed after a fight with his brother: "It's your fault, Mum, for reacting half an hour after it happened. You're like slime!" He was criticising me for not coming down on his brother at the time he hit him, but a while later.

Following brain injury, it is common to find that the person needs more time, often much more, to do normal things. This is because the neural pathways that were previously used are now affected by the brain injury, and other, less direct pathways must be used. It's like you're driving from home to work and you find that the main road you usually take is closed off, which means you have to take an alternative route that is not as direct and goes via a lot of small side streets. Of course, the journey time is significantly longer.

With spontaneous development, and even more so with rehabilitation, thanks to the brain's capacity for reorganisation, these side streets get wider and we can take shortcuts we never knew about. That way, we can reduce how long it takes, although we often can't be as quick as we used to be, because the main road was direct, and we can't use it anymore.

Chapter 3

Cognitive symptoms related to executive functions

Aurora Lassaletta and Amor Bize

Need for external guidance with organisation

For me, the main symptom of ABI, along with fatigue, is internal disorganisation, which manifests itself on a daily basis in external disorganisation. This symptom has been with me, and has been very apparent, from the beginning. It translates to an almost daily need for someone to help me to organise my everyday activities. At first, it was organisational help in all areas, and I am happy and grateful to remember my family carrying out this role when I was at my most dependent. Later, I still required this organisational support at home but, fortunately, over time I have needed it less. It is true that I am now able to perform many more tasks, albeit slowly, and that I get less tired than I used to. I have gained a lot of autonomy, but even so, I can't do without this support. I feel like I have had to change my personality in order to alleviate my new symptoms. If I want life to be less stressful, I now have to be more organised, more structured, more systematic. And that's not how I used to be.

Only my family and I know how much extra effort it takes for me to organise the house, how long I take to tidy up and how, in just a few minutes, I can mess it all up again and restore chaos: the fridge, the desk, the wardrobe . . . I think I could win a Guinness World Record for the fastest mess – at least that way I'd get something out of it! The daily work of trying not to return everything to chaos is massive, and sometimes I don't manage it, because I think it will be so hard that I put it off. This effort means going back to square one with tidying everything almost every day. It's as though two of my functions are failing: organisation and maintenance.

Without help, my house would be even more disorganised. When I want to tidy my wardrobe or one of the rooms, I stop to look around and see that my problem is not knowing where to start or what to do.

Problems with mental organisation are also reflected in not being able to keep the house tidy, even if someone else is doing it. It's like I've forgotten what order the steps go in. I accumulate things, because I don't really know what to do with them, and when I come to tidy up, I find myself moving piles of stuff from one place to another, unable to decide what to keep, what to throw away, or what to put in pride of place. The only advantage of not having any storage space is that I don't accumulate things in two different places! While it might sound like a joke, I seriously think that it would be easier for me to write a PhD thesis than to tidy my study.

> *Following brain injury, it is normal to see changes in executive functions, which are those responsible for managing our behaviour in relation to attaining a goal. To do this, these functions handle looking for targets, planning what steps to take, choosing suitable strategies and monitoring that we are doing everything in the right way to achieve them. One of the common consequences of this change is a difficulty being organised in situations that would previously have been handled automatically, and now require extra effort (Wilson, 1999).*

At home, my internal disorganisation is also apparent when I have to plan or make a meal. Every day I forget one of the steps I am supposed to take. I can give a perfect description of the logical steps this action requires in theory, in a quiet moment: organising a varied weekly menu; making a list and doing the shopping for that menu; arranging the food in the fridge and freezer according to the plan; defrosting whatever I need; and cooking, with or without help, what corresponds to that day. However, in practice it is not easy for me to remember them in order. It is as though this theory has not been internalised or automated. I can only remember all the steps if I back them up with some sort of external reminder. My smartphone functions as an external guide and gives me constant reminders. But sometimes, if I set too many reminders, I feel overwhelmed and I don't look at them.

> *It is common to find people with brain injury who are able to break down a complex activity into steps, if asked to do so in a session, but when they come to do the activity, they lose track of the sequence, forget one of the steps or do them out of order. This is due to their limited processing resources, which prevent them from accessing*

the mental plan while the steps are being taken, because there aren't enough resources for everything.

Since my internal organisation doesn't work, I am constantly trying to improve my external organisation. I buy folders for the bookshelf, wallets with compartments and cardholders for my handbag, lots of external tools to help me. This works for things I use less; for things I need every day, it might work for a day or two, but it won't be long before my bag goes back to being total chaos and my papers are all mixed up, disorganised and out of their folders. The same thing happens with Tupperware in the kitchen. I reorganised it, threw a lot away and was left with a few complete sets. Why can't I keep things tidy once I've organised them?

Having limited processing resources also means that, when they are performing an activity (for example organising a kitchen cupboard), people with brain injury cannot simultaneously keep track of where they are putting things and in which order they had planned to do it.

In addition to my organisational problems, I would also say I am not very realistic with planning. I keep planning more things than I am really able do. That's good as an incentive, but if there are too many things left to do it makes me more frustrated. Luckily, I keep learning and I don't try, as much as I used to, to fill every minute of the day with activities, but to get more enjoyment out of the few I do.

Planning the day's activities, for example, is a complex task that requires setting targets; thinking about how much time and what resources are needed to complete them; predicting what mood you will be in, or how tired, the circumstances around you; and fitting all that in with your own needs and those of your surroundings, etc. This makes it very common for people with brain injury not to do this realistically. People often plan things with the idea of themselves that they had before the brain injury (either because they lack awareness of their impairments, or because their memory has been affected), which leads them to overestimate their abilities.

What best reflects this internal disorganisation at the moment are my organisational efforts at the computer. Writing this book has been a real challenge, both in terms of communicating everything I've learned during the years, and organising the material. Knowing my problems, I asked a good friend to give me some tips and advice when it came to organising documents and folders on the computer, and to teach me how to transfer them to my tablet, so I could keep writing on there and replace the old document with the new one. Even with her advice and my utmost care, spending entire mornings just relocating and deleting things, I have duplicate files, whole paragraphs repeated in different places, information that I thought I had replaced, or lost . . . my computer desktop is a representation of my mind: total chaos!

When writing this book, it helped me to dedicate one morning each week exclusively to writing, although on many occasions I wasn't able to keep to that schedule.

I start a new notepad every time for meetings or courses about a particular topic; I tend to mix up the content of the notebooks and to not keep any logical order to what's inside. I can't stick to using the same document or notebook. For example, with this book, I have started several documents on the computer, which could have been a single file. The purpose was to write down things that I didn't know exactly where to put or that I was unsure whether to include or not. I don't know why, instead of adding to the first document, which was called "Mishmash", I started a second document, "For relocation", and then a third, "Miscellaneous for book", and even a fourth, "Where to put this in the book". And every time I revised a chapter to try to finish it, I had to remember to check all four documents, in case there was anything in them to be added to that particular chapter.

I never manage to take my referral note to a medical appointment. Yesterday I went to the hospital for a nutrition consultation, and I didn't have the note, as often happens. When I left, they gave me an appointment in six months' time. What I always do at this point is put it into the calendar on my mobile phone. That way I know I will definitely go to the appointment. The problem is not putting the appointment card in the appointments folder as soon as I get home. If I leave it anywhere else for a while, I won't be able to find it later.

Friends and family invite me to dinners and parties, and I really enjoy it, because it's important for me to socialise and spend time with people I feel comfortable around. I always offer to invite people over in return, but organising the house and dinners beyond the day-to-day is too much for me, and when I do it, I need a lot of technical help. I do intend to host them, but then I can't find a date. Once a year, on Mateo's birthday, I gather all my strength and both families, and with help, I organise a huge party at home. We all enjoy it and it's worth the effort, even though it leaves me exhausted for two days afterwards. The organisation of my fortieth birthday was a nice idea that never came to anything. It's so hard for me to act on a series of brilliant plans that seem so simple in my mind!

I have come to realise that internal disorganisation is complicated to recognise and understand from the outside. Sometimes, even I can't understand how it can be more difficult to organise the menu for the day than to sit down in my slow rhythm and translate a text from English to Spanish.

In many cases, cognitive functions are independent of one another. For example, translation from one language to another might be easier for someone who is bilingual, because in this activity they don't need to hold the same amount of data and variables in their head in advance, just to remember the meaning of the word and write it down. Planning, however, means keeping your mind on targets, resources, strategies and personal and environmental circumstances, and that requires a significant amount of working memory.

I get the feeling that, from the outside, it might seem like my messiness is just down to me being lazy or unwilling. And I'm sure it does have something to do with that, but not exclusively. I have never been very tidy, but I always had the means, which I no longer have, to sort things out quickly and keep them that way.

Several times over the last few years, I have changed the people who help me with the house or with looking after the children, and I think these changes relate to the role I need the person to take in my household. Really, I need someone who can organise things by themselves, without me having to manage them. It's like I can't be the captain of my own ship and I need that person to take the helm. The continuity problems with people providing domestic help, relationships that have been ended by both sides, relate to this issue. I think that, for the person who comes in to help me, it can be difficult to understand that I am at home, not going out to work, and I don't know how to organise myself. I'm sure this would be easier if I were in a wheelchair.

I need to find people to take over my roles who can adapt to me once they know my situation. Fortunately, in some cases I have found people who could do this: taking into account my difficulties, compensating for my lack of improvisation by preparing a meal if I had forgotten to tell them to, making a list of things I need to buy, or even sewing some clothes, if need be.

To help someone with organisational problems, it takes someone who understands their changes and who has a good dose of initiative, and that can be difficult to find (Wilson, Evans, Gracey and Bateman, 2009).

Despite lacking drive, it makes me happy to organise something for other people sometimes, even though I then can't organise myself. It's very typical of me to send an email to remind everyone to take toys for disadvantaged children to a well-known children's toy shop when it is running a collection campaign. I spread the word, everyone thanks me and lots of people take along their toys. But when I get ready to take my own toys, the date has already passed.

I also successfully arranged a bus trip for a large group of people to go from Madrid to an event near Burgos, and everyone was very grateful because it made things much easier for them. I did each stage calmly, at my own pace. I got a good price, but on the day, I mistimed my journey and arrived late to the departure point. For a while, the group didn't have a captain – which is exactly how I feel!

I have stopped half way through important rehabilitation processes, as in the case of my eye or my shoulder, when, because of my normal appearance, the rehabilitation therapists think that I can do it alone at home. That is the moment when I abandon rehabilitation, although I'm not aware that that's what I'm doing at the time. It is costly in many ways to make daily trips for someone to guide my rehabilitation, but not doing it by myself is not only a question of motivation, but also, once again, of my internal organisation. Discipline is closely related to this problem. It's not that I'm lazy or uninterested in regaining the movement in my eye; however, I am unable to organise and plan a moment to put the rehabilitation exercises into action by myself.

The best way to face this difficulty is to be very conscious of it.

I can say that I am increasingly independent in many of my day-to-day activities. I am very lucky not to have a physical dependency, like when someone had to push my wheelchair around, but I do still have a "neuropsychological" dependency, as I call it, in this need for external guidance. Because in reality my organisation, although it has improved somewhat, continues to be quite chaotic, and I can't limit that chaos. I had always got along fine, because I had a lot of resources for dealing with chaotic situations. Now I don't have those resources and unless I prepare for it, chaos gets the better of me and everyone around me. I live with my family in a very lively apartment, which is hard for me to organise.

Even when it came to doing my daily Pilates exercises, I decided to ask the teacher to make an audio recording so I could remember the steps. Often, because my day is so disorganised, I can't find a gap to do these exercises, or I don't even remember to do them, but when I do I really benefit from that external guide.

When I'm packing suitcases, I sometimes forget to put in the most important thing. I make lists and then forget to check them. As it's so hard for me to decide which clothes are important, I tend to pack very heavy suitcases. It makes me laugh to think of my mother, who knows this problem well, always offering her well-intentioned advice to pack light.

I feel like it might be a good idea for me to go back to school now, with a good teacher who could set me specific tasks at specific times. Perhaps that way I would avoid the frustration of ending the week without having been able to do many of the things I'd had planned.

> *The best way to help a "disorganised" person is by structuring activities in their everyday life in routines that are as stable as possible. Only with fixed timetables can the person distribute their limited resources to other tasks and not have to think about what to do when (Wilson, Evans, Gracey and Bateman, 2009).*

Planning and managing free time with my family is not one of my fortes, either. Luckily, that responsibility doesn't lie only with me, and we plan and improvise things together as much as we can.

This morning, I was thinking that if I wrote a letter to Father Christmas, I would ask him to lend me one of his elves for a while to help me organise the fridge, another to organise my wardrobe and another to tidy the kitchen! Sometimes I imagine that the only way to solve my disorganisation at home would be to call a moving company and have them clear all the shelves and cupboards in the house, put everything in little boxes so that I could go through them bit by bit, organising sections or groups of things. That would be much easier for me, in sections, than facing it all at once. Although I honestly don't know how long it would stay tidy!

I make the most of weekends and quiet moments when I don't have to stick to timetables or schedules to organise things bit by bit, even though I do it very slowly.

A particularly good example of my need for external guidance was online mindfulness training. It was important for me to make meditation practice into a habit. The training process began with 30 consecutive sessions, one each day, and they were guided. I needed that guidance, and I was delighted that there was only one way to do it, and for one month I knew which training session I was on that day. Usually, I would sit down in the same place, with my headphones on and my eyes closed, to do my practice. I always did it, even if I changed the place or time, it became "sacred" to me. At the end of session number 30, there was no longer only one way; you could choose from different packages of sessions to focus on a particular theme. It was all optional. I shuffled from one theme to another, without spending much time on any of them. I went back through the first block of 30 sessions, but with less motivation. And when I lost the external guide, my practice faded out. I disproved the theory that 21 days of practising or repeating something is all it takes to implement a change!

What I do now is plan events for the quarter and review them every month. I often ask Nacho to check whether the plans are realistic. He knows what I'm like, and is all too familiar with the consequences of me overstretching myself. Sometimes he'll laugh and say that I'm obsessed with calendars because I have several in different rooms, but in reality I need them, as well as the reminders in my mobile phone.

Complicated decision-making

Over the years, I have noticed that I have tremendous difficulty making decisions and sticking to them. At first, I thought that my personality had changed, because I had always been quite a positive, quick, "best foot forward" kind of person and, in general, once I had made a decision I wouldn't go back on it. I never thought of myself as particularly obsessive, and now I find I get stuck in repetitive thought patterns. I am gradually realising that my personality hasn't changed, but the way I think has altered, as has the way I approach decisions. After observing myself and listening to what my family tell me, I realise that my thought process is very often circular, and this new way of thinking is usually involuntary. I strongly support C. Osborn in her mission to raise the visibility of the consequences that a head trauma has on problem-solving and decision-making abilities since – as she explains in her book– what is a simple act for most people takes a huge conscious effort for someone affected by brain injury (Osborn, 2000).

I go over and over things in my head and I'm never sure what I've decided. Before, while I would dwell on things sometimes, I used to make decisions much more quickly and practically, and move on to something else. Now my head won't stop! I know that this isn't easy for me or my family who are with me day-to-day, especially when I'm making a decision and look at all the pros and cons, then take the opposite view, again with pros and cons, and even a third option with the same analysis. It's exhausting spending all day with your brain switched to "ON"!

Sometimes people with brain injury have difficulty "wiping the slate clean" when they have finished a task. There seems to be a change in how they manage processing resources, which means that they keep elements (ideas, words, problems) active when they should really have deactivated them. Particularly if it is something complex or worrying for the person and therefore a lot of resources have been assigned to solving the problem, these resources will continue to activate the information even though this is no longer necessary.

It's strange to think that, while I have a strong tendency to be physically passive, my thoughts, although slower, are sometimes desperately active. My aim is to try to switch off, not to be alert, and to relax my mind. The relaxation and mediation sessions do me good in the short term, at least to stop me getting bogged down in my own thoughts. This practice requires organisation, scheduling and discipline that is easy in quiet moments, and more complicated at chaotic times.

At some points, this symptom has also been diagnosed as "subthreshold depression", and, of course, if I'm in low spirits it gets worse, but with time both the professionals and I have realised that this is not the only determining factor. When I consulted the neuropsychologist about this problem for the first time, she told me about dysexecutive syndrome, and explained that these circles and repetitions are often described in this condition. It really helped me to find out about it and know why it's like this, although I don't feel like it's very easy to change. Most of all, it helped me not to be too critical of myself for this behaviour.

> *Dysexecutive syndrome covers a multitude of symptoms relating to problems with organising, planning, supervising and monitoring behaviour (Goldstein and Beers, 1998).*

I remember, as if it were way back in time, the difficult selection of tiles for our house. My accident coincided with a major fault that called for a full refurbishment of the bathroom and kitchen. It wasn't a good time for extra costs, but we had no choice but to get on with it. I admire Nacho's decision-making and the way he went ahead with everything at that point. As I was recovering physically, there came a day when he found himself overwhelmed and asked me to help him decide which tiles to buy, by doing a quality/price review. We went to the shop; I stopped in front of each tile display on my crutches, and I was absolutely incapable of deciding on anything. I couldn't even imagine what a whole room would look like with those tiles.

Making a decision uses a lot of processing resources, because you have to keep in mind each and every one of the options available, with its pros and cons (price, aesthetics, quality, etc.), to be able to decide which is the best.

I'm sure that I had extra neurological fatigue in this situation, and there were plenty of other symptoms present, but it was the first time that neither Nacho nor I could understand why I wasn't able to make a quick, easy decision the way I had always done. The tiles that I look at every day in my house are the result of a snap decision made by my husband because I had a complete mental block.

Several years later, in one of life's coincidences, a friend asked me to go and give advice on which tiles to buy for her house. That time I was able to do it properly, taking into account all the things I have learned over time. The first thing I did was apply my favourite motto, "just one intense thing a day!", and I told my friend that we should go on different days to choose the tiles for different rooms. I don't know whether she understood that request, but fortunately she respected it. The day before we went, I did an intense internet search on different models, so that I had more or less the idea of which kind of tiles I liked. And the next day I accompanied my friend to two or three shops. She has always said that my advice helped her to come to a decision. I remember it as a very intense mental process, but because I watched my limits, I also remember making the right decisions as a really satisfying feeling.

I'm sure that my difficulties with decision-making and thinking in circles are closely related to other symptoms. Of course, it's not going to be easy making decisions with a disorganised mind that struggles to pay attention, can't distinguish between priorities and non-essentials, often forgets things and doesn't know how to get to the point. Put like that, it sounds quite dramatic!

Decision-making brings into play the functions of attention, memory, thought and, of course, executive functions.

Luckily, and as I have said in several chapters, it has been essential for me to learn the tools of planning and scheduling, which are also a big help with important decisions, like summer holidays, the children's camps and extracurricular activities or priority expenses. With all these things, I take my time, I write down all the options, the pros and cons of each option and the variables. Sharing this with Nacho helps us to make the best possible decision.

When we make a good plan, we can relieve our working memory (the capacity to keep active and manipulate information with the mind) and allocate these resources to making the decision itself (reasoning).

I have happy memories of making decisions about our summer holiday in Ireland. An invitation to stay with some good Irish friends is something I'll never forget, and which helped us to plan an adventure that would otherwise not have been possible. Following the invitation, we decided that we wanted the trip to support our sons' English studies. Slowly, and with a lot of work, I was able to find, choose and plan various free or very cheap activities for all members of the family, which turned out very well. People told me it was incredible the amount of organisation and decision-making I had done to prepare three weeks of English for the whole family. I know that what really helped was dedicating almost five months to making all the decisions slowly, carefully writing down the possible plans and asking for help when it got too much for me. But I'm also really proud of the great result of all this meticulous work.

For quicker decisions, I often surprise myself by thinking in circles. But I have decided first of all to trust my intuition which, although it makes me a bit insecure, also gives good results. And here I'm like most parents: sometimes we get it wrong, but most of the time we get it right!

At the moment, for tasks like choosing a household appliance, I find times when I'm most relaxed and periods during the day when there aren't many people in the shops, like in the mornings, so I can avoid the noise and fuss and stress. So that I don't stand staring blankly at all the microwaves in the shop, I do most of the work on the computer at home. Who'd have thought I would find it easier to choose a microwave in quiet moments than a shower head surrounded by stress!

Difficulty adapting to changes

I have always been a very adaptable person; I've lived in different countries and different houses, driven different cars, travelled and encountered far-away places and met very different people who became my friends. Now, however, I prefer to be in a familiar or structured environment, as I need things around me to stay the same and not change too much. It's not easy for me to deal with someone new supervising my sports activities or rehabilitation, and I take a long time to adjust to new people. More significant changes, like someone new helping me with domestic tasks, affect me even more and cause significant internal disorganisation.

People who suffer brain injury have fewer cognitive resources to deal with change. Getting out of a routine means implementing a new plan of action, "recognising" the new thing and adapting to it, whether this is a person, a bus journey or a kitchen. This means that you can't function using the system you know: processes that were once automatic (because they have been repeated many times) now have to be conscious, with the increase in resources that that requires. We can understand that the direct consequence will be that the tendency to become tired appears earlier and is more intense.

This is at odds with my old personality, because I used to love surprises, novelty, new people and new places. And I still have part of that personality, especially my desire to travel and see new sights and new faces, but I can only recover this side of my personality on holiday or at very relaxed times. During the school year, I need more routine, since too many new things leave me immediately saturated. Being aware of this strict regime, I now try to test out small changes in day-to-day life. When there are several possible routes home from somewhere, like the children's school, or choir, if I'm calm and relaxed, I will normally choose a different route each time. For holidays, or travel, I have tried to adapt to new places, like I used to, but I recognise that it is much easier for me to enjoy myself if I spend a few days in a hotel or a guest house where I don't need to cook, than to rent an apartment where my organisational problems cause me extra stress.

We are all familiar with the recommendation to "move outside our comfort zone" to stimulate the brain and set ourselves new challenges. However, we also need to have the necessary cognitive resources because, otherwise, we will force a person with brain injury to face a situation that is too much for them and that will probably increase their sense of frustration and irascibility.

Robberies, from what many people have told me, leave considerable and long-lasting anxiety. We suffered a robbery at home some years ago and for several months I had the feeling that everything had been thrown into disarray inside me, as well as in the house. After almost a year, I finally managed to sit down and go back to writing the book. It was losing my tools and my workspace – they stole my desktop computer and my laptop – along with tidying and reorganising the house, which for anyone else is an external problem but for me is also an internal problem, that made it very difficult to adapt to the change. More than ever, I felt like I was missing the planning and decision-making tools required for the difficult task of tidying and reorganising.

My smartphone plays an important role for me as an organiser. My son Álvaro, who is my technician and technical assistant, told me one day that my telephone was now obsolete and I couldn't update it anymore, and recommended that I should change it. A few months after changing my mobile phone, I've got the hang of the new one after a long and difficult adjustment but, if I had to choose, I would still rather the old one.

Impaired creativity

My lack of initiative or tendency to stillness is also reflected in my feeling that I generate few new ideas. I feel like my mind is now a bit more rigid, less flexible. It's as though I only feel at ease with what I've always known, and can't make space for new things.

With the notes I've been writing to remind myself of ideas that came to me for the book, I have been able to see how I would always write them in the same way, using the same words; even years later I was repeating them precisely, without ever remembering that I had already written about the same thing.

> *Divergent thinking means thinking that establishes criteria of originality, inventiveness and flexibility. Following brain injury, it is common to find that the person is unable to deviate from their usual pattern, which makes it harder to find new solutions to complex problems. Creativity calls for more cognitive resources than following a known system. It means assessing the objective and implementing alternatives that hadn't been thought of before.*

If I didn't set myself the task, I would almost never change my clothes, handbag, coat or shoes. I always put on clean clothes and I don't neglect my personal hygiene, but I'm not inspired to vary my look. Once I made a therapeutic effort and went to buy some new clothes, but I forgot about them and left them in the bag for over a year. Personally, I would happily wear some sort of uniform that stopped me wasting energy on deciding how to vary my outfits, and if I were getting my children's clothes ready every day, I would do something similar. The good thing is that they're growing up and starting to make their own choices.

The same thing happens to me sometimes with food, and my family complain about getting the same meals – they want more variety. As I'm the only one who cooks, or if they help me I have to decide what we're eating, at home I ask them for ideas, because nothing different occurs to me at the time. It's like my variety neurons have been affected!

The children are my masters. Mateo will say "Mum, pleeease, change the snacks. Not ham and cheese sandwiches every time! Some days you can put in biscuits, some days cake bars, but never fruit, ok?" The positive outcome is that I asked him to help me to make the weekly snack menu and we have fun planning it.

Luckily, I've been able to recognise that this happens to me, and I solve it by choosing quiet moments at the weekend to plan different meals for the coming days. I look at recipe websites online and see lots of variation that gives me ideas. Similarly, I open the wardrobe before I get dressed and look at the clothes in there – that way I can see all the options and it's much easier to think of combinations and variations. Sometimes, if I really try, I can even go too far! The other day, my children told me that they had never eaten such an interesting rice salad with so many different ingredients.

My mother, seeing me dress in very similar clothes all the time, went with me during the holidays to buy new clothes and bought me three pairs of trousers and a handbag that I loved. One pair of trousers was slightly more comfortable than the other two, so the following day I gave them their debut, with the idea that from then on I would start to change them up. It makes me laugh now to realise that I just repeated the pattern: the new trousers have become my new favourite uniform and I wear them every day; I only change them on laundry day, when I reluctantly put on the old ones. The new pair has replaced the old pair, but my inertia has stayed just the same.

Difficulty generating new ideas also affects communication and social relationships. I was interested to read about treatments using tools to compensate for this impairment. The treatment of one patient, Eliot, consisted of being able to plan various conversation topics so that, when he was in social situations, this residual disability did not leave him blocked and excluded (Wilson, Winegardner and Ashworth, 2014). After fourteen years, I still struggle to fully grasp the concept of "executive functions", although I am very familiar with the symptoms I live with every day. Recently I have been helped by reading Christopher Yeoh's book where he explains them as the highest-level mental processes (Yeoh, 2018).

Chapter 4

Cognitive symptoms related to memory

Aurora Lassaletta and Amor Bize

Memory difficulty: the need for "cognitive crutches"

My memory has been affected since the TBI, but in a peculiar way, which I struggle to understand. There are a few things that I can't remember (fortunately I do remember the important things), and the memories I have are often disordered. Seeing much more serious memory problems in people around me and in what I have read, I now realise the extent of the problems serious memory impairments can have on resuming your daily routine and social life after a sudden brain injury. I was particularly struck by the metaphor used by Christopher Yeoh, writing about the early stages when he had just come out of a coma, who likens his memory to a revolving door in which any information that comes in immediately goes out (Yeoh, 2018).

> *Following brain injury it is very common to experience memory issues that are often related to attention problems that prevent or hinder the proper coding (processing) of information (what is happening) and, consequently, the person struggles to remember (Wilson, 2009).*

Like older people, I often have more detailed memories of things from the past than those that happened just a month ago, but in general my memory allows me to manage day-to-day life – that is, with tools that help me to remember. According to my children, I also repeat things several times. This is sometimes because I forget what I've already said, but very often I'm just being insistent, like any mother. However, some memory failings, which are more subtle but just as important, can only be avoided if I really concentrate. Some of them affect my health, like forgetting to care for my physical symptoms; others affect my bank account, like buying things in duplicate at different times.

Following brain injury, it is common for anterograde memory to be affected, which is memory that relates to learning and remembering data and events that take place after *the injury. Retrograde memory, which concerns autobiographical information and general knowledge acquired* before *the injury, is usually better preserved (Baddeley, Kopelman and Wilson, 2002).*

The trauma specialist told me that, because of my back injuries, it was important to wear a special corset for sports, but when I go to paddle tennis classes with the Brain Injury Sports Club, I forget it practically every time. Only later, when my back is hurting, will I remember that I haven't worn it. This consequence should be enough to remind me to wear it the following week, but it isn't. Since there's no specific reminder in my mobile phone for the right moment, before I leave the house, I completely forget it. Even though I have back pain almost every day!

In Ireland, after staying with our friends, we travelled around for a weekend and got to know a beautiful section of the coast. I had planned it, searching well in advance for accommodation that was cheap and highly recommended. There was an online reservation system with free cancellation up to 48 hours in advance, and as I was organising everything three months ahead of time, I decided to book two different bed and breakfasts for the same weekend. I didn't know which would be closer to the bus stop where we arrived, and this way I could cancel one of them when we got to Ireland and found out. But I completely forgot to do that, and I was so annoyed when I got a phone call in Ireland from the accommodation that we hadn't used, asking why we hadn't arrived the night before and informing me that we had been charged for the night.

Sometimes I park the car in a regulated parking zone, and I completely forget to pay for it. I will only remember when I come back from my shopping or meeting to find a parking ticket. And as if anyone could make parking attendants understand my cognitive difficulties! I solve these memory problems with extra analysis and continuous awareness, which I often find exhausting.

Difficulties with remembering what we have to do in the future (prospective memory) are closely related to limited processing resources and poor management of these resources, which means that, if attention is focused on one task, there aren't enough resources left to keep the thing we need to remember active, i.e. not to forget it (Wilson, 2009).

My friends used to call me the "Musical Encyclopaedia", because when we sang, I would always know the words to all the songs. I found it easy to learn and remember the words quickly. Now I can't remember the songs I used to know at all, and it takes a lot of effort for me to remember the new ones I learn. At choir, despite having improved my attention and memory a lot over the years, I have real difficulty remembering the words to songs. Before, we used to sing with the words in front of us, but lately we have been asked to memorise the songs carefully, to sing without music stands or scores. I am terrible at that. There are a few songs that I just can't get, and no matter how much I repeat them, at the moment of truth in the concert I might go blank and have to mime. Sometimes I have to resort to tricks from my school days, like writing notes on my hand!

Besides limitations at the first stage of learning (coding or processing information), the memory can also be altered by difficulties at the second stage: storage. This way, despite carrying out suitable processing of what we want to learn, the imprint left on the memory is not strong enough and the information can disappear a few minutes after processing.

Emotions have a strong influence on this function. If I'm nervous at a concert or I haven't rested enough, my memory is much more affected.

Our emotions play a very clear role in learning and memory. In principle, if the event or information to be remembered has an emotional value for the person, it should be more easily recorded in their memory. However, if the emotional repercussions cross a certain threshold, this hyperactivation will make coding and storing the information more difficult, which often happens with traumatic events.

Even now, when I'm at my best, I still come up against little memory problems that annoy me. I don't think I was, or am, very aware of these memory problems. One particularly relevant example is writing this book. I would like to describe what has been happening, and is still happening to me, when I write. When I get an idea for the book, I jot it down straight away. At those moments, I am very happy with the idea, with how novel it seems to me, and I go over it, writing down the details quickly so I don't forget anything and can flesh them out later. This is the system I use: when I get an idea – wherever it might be, in the street, on the bus, waiting for my kids to come out school – I quickly note down the main ideas or key words, or record them on my phone. Later, looking at these words, I can develop the idea. I note down on my phone, in a notebook, or sometimes on a piece of paper, different ideas, or what I think are different ideas. It has surprised me, and it still surprises me very much to find ideas for the book written down four or five times, years apart, told in a very similar way in different notes, experiencing them on each occasion as if it were the first time they had occurred to me.

I have noticed several examples with this book. I sit down to write and I come up with a strategy to use different colours, where each one means something different ("revised", "recently added", "undecided", etc.) When I haven't noted down the meaning of the colours, I have found myself going back to the writing some time later and not understanding anything. It makes no difference whether the colours are there or not if I can't remember what the colours mean. Now I have created a fantastic document called "Colour Guide" that explains the meaning of each colour, which I check every time I'm revising something I have written. With this information, I don't get stuck.

I was recently reminded of the limitations of my memory when I tried to remember how the idea of writing this book came about in the first place. No matter how hard I tried, I couldn't remember and that worried me, until I came up with the strategy, after several days of trying to force the memory, of looking for the email I sent to my group of friends telling them I was going to write the book. That's where I found the explanation I gave them of why I was setting myself this task, and how the idea had arisen and developed.

It is very common for people to be unaware of their own memory limitations. And this is logical, because to become aware of something we need a series of episodes where we have experienced the limitations. However, due to the very nature of memory changes, this information cannot be recalled, which means that the person does not suffer the frustration of recognising their difficulty, which would help them to be aware of it.

The same thing happens with tidying the house. Saving something important and then finding it again becomes mission impossible.

The problem is that, when I'm putting something in a safe place, I really do believe that I will remember it without any problems. That is the real limitation: the lack of awareness of the memory impairment. Later, when I want to find it, I can't remember for the life of me where I put it, and stressful situations repeat themselves time and again, moments of total chaos when I'm searching for something. This is why I came up with the plan to keep a notebook listing where I have put important things. As well as having them in writing on my bookshelf, I also have my notes copied on my smartphone, which means that I can find them quickly and easily. You need a good memory to be well organised!

> *Similar to other superior cognitive functions, memory and executive functions ("the boss" of the system) feed into one another, which means that, without good organisation and planning of information, it will be impossible to store and remember it properly; on the other hand, if you can't remember the compensatory strategies or tricks to get along more independently, "the boss" will be completely ineffective.*

Last week, I thought about making a stew for dinner the next day, because it had been a while since I last cooked one. Then I had the great idea of buying a pre-prepared packet of stew vegetables. Luckily, as part of my task, I checked the fridge before I went shopping, and to my surprise I opened the vegetable box to find a packet exactly like the one I was about to buy, which had expired the previous day, meaning I must have bought it two weeks earlier. I realise how helpful my new checking routine is, but if I have to do the shopping at a moment when my passivity takes over, or on a day when I have already been "too disciplined", and I can't improvise, I don't check, and accidentally buy things that I already have at home. In these cases, all I can do is accept it – laugh about it if I can, and get annoyed if I can't.

Until recently, I would often find clothes, shoes and other items that I had bought and completely forgotten about just left in storage. A very nice pair of boots, which I bought in a sale and put in a cupboard, were found two years later. I've done it with clothes, lotions, gifts. I have even bought things in duplicate because I couldn't remember that I'd already bought them. When this kept happening, I decided to stick little lists on the outside of the drawers or shelves in the cupboards at home, including a copy in the packed notes section of my mobile, and that helps me a lot. Of course, my family are a bit sick of being asked to keep things tidy, especially when I can't even do it myself!

Organising daily activities and establishing routines is essential for making sure people with memory changes can cope independently (Wilson, Herbert and Shiel, 2003).

This new strategy has helped me a lot, because I often find that I can't remember what clothes I own. I might think that I don't have any smart dresses for a wedding when I actually bought one a year earlier for another wedding. I can't remember my clothes at all, or the children's. Last year, I bought the boys some trousers for a family wedding, and two months later I found almost identical trousers that I had bought a year earlier for a different event. Luckily, my way of dealing with these incidents has become more optimistic. My first thought is: "I'm sure I have something for the wedding, I just can't remember it now, I'll check my lists". Sometimes I get angry when I then discover that I really don't have anything!

I love wearing pendants or necklaces, but the same thing was happening: I almost always picked out the same one or forgot what I had. I bought a very stylish metal tree where I can keep them all hanging in view. I put it in the bathroom and that helps me to vary things a little bit more.

Constantly losing things is another consequence of this memory problem. Today I spent a long time looking for a recipe book where I keep important recipes, and I couldn't find it, which meant I couldn't cook the dish I wanted to make. This happens to me all the time. I solve it by making more effort to keep things tidy. It's been great for me to buy about twenty coloured folders from IKEA, which have labels on the outside where I've written what they contain. Out of respect for my internal chaos, I allowed myself to keep one called "VARIOUS", which lets me throw things in there in a disorganised way – paper or things that I don't have the time or mental capacity to organise. If I can't find a paper, it's one of the first places I look.

I realise that memory and organising information are closely related. I do remember a lot of details about events, especially important and past ones, but often I'm unable to remember the sequence of what came before or after. To get it back, I've had to ask other people for dates and details. I'm noting them down to make a graphic timeline of my life. Before, every time anyone asked, "Do you remember when . . .?", I would get tense and feel bad, because very often I couldn't remember the situation they were talking about. Now it doesn't affect me as much. Fortunately, I know that I can remember the important things, although there's a whole series of details where I have to ask for hints or photos to help me get my memories back. In his book, Christopher Yeoh apologises for any confusion that may be caused by reading his memories out of order; at the same time, he asks the reader to put themselves in the shoes of someone who has an ABI (Yeoh, 2018).

The strategy of using external tools to compensate for functions that I can't regain in full is something I learned at CEADAC and, when it comes to memory problems, and above all organisational problems, it has helped me a lot. In my day-to-day life, the reminders on my smartphone, and the daily, weekly and monthly calendars help me to remember what I need to do. Without the sound of the reminder, it would be no help to keep a diary with everything noted down, because I would forget to look at it. At home, everyone's so used to it that, as soon as Mateo started talking, whenever he heard the alarm he would say, "Mum, reminders!" Technological advances really have been an enormous advantage for me at this time. I don't know what I would have had to come up with twenty years ago!

Keeping a diary has really helped me to see my development over the years. Professionals recommend a diary for memory (Winson, Wilson and Bateman, 2017) and I also recommend a general diary where you can pour out your feelings. I think it can help to work many functions together, and it's good for their development as well as for awareness of deficits and the emotional process. This exercise of seeing yourself from the outside when you read the diary has been very useful to me. Writing by hand, instead of on a computer or electronic device, also has the advantage of working psychomotricity (Denton, 2008). Reading what their patients have written can offer professionals important insights into the subjective experience of their deficits and recovery (Easton and Atkin, 2011).

I had to have an extra set of keys cut and keep them in the lock, because at the very moment I need to leave, I'll often be desperately hunting for keys and unable to find them or remember where I left them. Now, when I'm in a rush, I can take this spare set. Most of the time, when I get home and look carefully, I find that the original keys are also in my bag, but it's a big comfort to know that I have another set with me and can lock the door from the outside.

Attention and memory are closely related. I can't really remember anything that I haven't paid much attention to, but, again, I think I can say that memory problems are not only dependent on that. An experience comes to mind that confirms this idea: in the summer, in a relaxed holiday environment, a friend told us part of his family story that I didn't know. It was a very special, personal and interesting tale that grabbed my full attention. I was very glad that he shared it with us and I kept thinking about the story for a few days. Now, four months later, I realise that I can't remember it, and in this case that has nothing to do with my attention, it has to be something else.

It is much easier to realise that a person who has mobility problems because of an ABI needs help with walking than to tell that many of us need what I have started to call "cognitive crutches". In 2018 I had two experiences that made me very aware of the need for these cognitive crutches. I was asked to take part in a documentary about people who had suffered an ABI and they wanted to film some scenes of me writing my blog. They told me that during filming they would ask questions that I would not be given in advance. I was so surprised when I was asked a very obvious question: "What are the main side effects you have been left with?" I went blank and was only able to remember tiredness. You can imagine my frustration after the filming!

Once again, following my method of observing and analysing this impairment and gathering information from other professionals, I have realised that this memory problem is related to access to information. This impairment is shared by many people with ABI and there are tools than can help us to avoid it. I remembered about children with ABI at school and their difficulties when faced with open questions in exams. The same thing had happened to me! Quiz style exams are easier, because it's not that children don't remember the information. The information is there, but they need a few key words that give a link to the information: "cognitive crutches". After the filming, I thought that perhaps if I had been able to look at the contents page of my book, and see the titles of each chapter, it would have awakened the information I needed and it would have been enough for me to talk for half-an-hour about each impairment. The contents page would have been my tool.

My next experience would be a live 30-minute radio interview. I wasn't given the questions in advance on that occasion, either. I was wondering whether I should explain the problem that some people with ABI have with accessing information, and ask them to send me the questions so I didn't go blank when faced with an open question. But in the end I decided to treat it as a challenge and prepare my tools to make sure that didn't happen. I spent a few days making a summary of what I thought was important, and even an extended contents page from my book, in case they asked me about that. In short bursts, because of the saturation it caused, I was preparing my "cognitive crutches", and when I got there, I felt the security of having my summary in front of me with all the references I needed, and I could expand on them quite well. Now

I have learned how I need to approach this kind of situation to work around my impairment, and I can do it with less stress.

> *The functions of learning and memory have three basic phases, which can be altered independently following a brain injury:*
>
> 1 *Coding and processing information.*
> 2 *Storage.*
> 3 *Recovering or remembering information.*
>
> *Obviously, if information is not suitably coded, it cannot be stored or recovered. This change would relate to attention deficits. Other times, however, data is processed but the memory imprint (storage) fails, which means it is not remembered. This would affect "pure" memory.*
>
> *Lastly, the information might be coded and stored adequately, but there are no effective strategies for recovering the information. In this case, we are talking about the most "executive" component of memory, and it can be facilitated by offering key phonetics ("it begins with 'S'") or semantics ("it's one of your favourite foods") (Baddeley, Kopelman and Wilson, 2002).*

Another resource I often use to compensate for memory problems are photos on my phone. I take pictures of everything and keep all kinds of things on there: payment dates for the children's swimming, my box of cheap jewellery, the inside of the fridge, newsletters that my children bring home from school or tupperware boxes that my mother or my mother-in-law sometimes give me food in, so that I know which is which and can return them later.

I have put a coat rack in my bedroom where I hang many of my handbags, so that when I see them I remember that they exist. Even so, since a handbag changeover takes a while and calls for extra order and organisation, it makes me laugh when I see myself in the mirror in the hallway all year round carrying the same brightly coloured bag, a present from a good friend. My reflection says to me "again!" It's not just an excuse, but my favourite bag, as well as being like a sack where everything ends up, is my only bag that has a hook inside for keys so I can't lose them, and when I do remember to clip them on, it spares me a long time hunting around for them in the hallway and in the front door.

I've realised that, if I want to commit something that I have read to memory and recall it later, I can't read it quickly, or even quite quickly – the way

I used to – because I can't take in information that way anymore. I recently wanted to explain to a friend what Sanfilippo syndrome was, because a month and half earlier my son and I had quickly read a plan to help research into this rare disease, which we wanted to support. I was perplexed when I couldn't explain anything about the syndrome, because at the time I hadn't spent long looking at it in depth.

There are some things I feel worse about forgetting, like sending photos of the teacher's house that they were able to build in an inaccessible village with no school in Burkina Faso, thanks to a project I worked on with great interest four years ago. I met with various people, explained the project and collected financial donations. I always think that all those people who contributed would be happy to see the finished house, but something as simple as that was always forgotten, or passed me by, or was difficult to organise at times when I did remember it.

Sometimes it helps to arrange your to-do list in a table like this:

	URGENT	*NON-URGENT*
IMPORTANT		
UNIMPORTANT		

This way, you can plan activities in your diary, prioritising what is urgent and important.

I'll read a book and very quickly forget the details. I remember books more easily when I connect with them emotionally, perhaps not the content but the feelings they transmit. The one that springs to mind was the first book I managed to read after three years; it was my challenge and I loved it, although it was emotionally tough. It was *The Kite Runner* by Khaled Hosseini. At the time of writing, I was reading *Wonder* by R. J. Palacio in English, which I had read in Spanish the previous summer and loved. I do remember what it's about, the characters and the emotions, but because I can't remember the details, it feels like reading a new book. The same thing often happens with films. To make an effort to remember them, sometimes I try to give someone a summary of the book or film at the end. Writing the summary down would be a good tactic but I'm still not in the habit.

Occasionally, I have forgotten that I have left the fire or the oven on for a while, so I always have to work with alarms. As a strategy to prevent this sort of forgetfulness, it has been very helpful for me to buy a cooking pot that can be programmed with very specific times, and turns off by itself, and I use the electric kettle to keep me constantly supplied with tea.

My most significant recent loss was the pen drive where I kept this book backed up. I still don't know how I lost it, and I have looked everywhere for it – a common occurrence now, even with very important things. This didn't happen to me before.

Slow learning curve

Despite feeling like I now have a smaller "hard drive" due to my TBI, I am still learning new things, more slowly and with a bit more effort.

I have always tried to keep stimulating my brain and learning. I've spent several years trying to resume reading in English, starting with children's books and then moving on to simple novels. I am still trying to read more complex things, even though this is difficult. I do the same, sometimes, with a TV series or programme that I can put on in English. I don't want to hit a plateau, but instead to keep making progress, setting myself challenges from which I can learn.

With my children, I have been learning school topics; I have attended training days in certain areas of psychology that interest me; and of course I have kept learning in various neurofunctional rehabilitation programmes. To learn properly, I feel like the world would need to turn at fewer revolutions per minute; to understand a film in English now, or to follow an interesting talk, I would need it to be slower. This is because I process information slowly. But another problem is that this learning, as well as taking so much effort, does not last long. Like other people affected by brain injury, I am still aware of the difficulty in retaining what I have learned (Roberts, 2014). Since I forget things more easily, I have to choose carefully the most important things on which to focus my attention. For specific information I use the rules of mnemonics, which are creative and help me to remember everything from email passwords to the name of a new physiotherapist.

> *Following brain injury, the resources for processing information are limited and this means that learning processes slow down or begin to require more effort. This is because of a failure with information coding (attention) or storage (memory), or with recovering or remembering what has been learned (executive component) (Christensen and Uzzell, 1999).*

I sometimes have to study choir songs as if they were a history topic at school, and repeat them, write them down and recite them over and over. Mateo helps by testing me on what I've studied, and we make it fun. Doing little administrative jobs on the computer – things I have helped my brother with – I realise that if I don't record or write down how to do each thing as I do it, the next time he needs my help, even if it's just six months later, I will already have forgotten and need to learn everything again from scratch. It's as though the "easy recall of things I already know" function, which we all normally have, is not working. And this means making an extra effort to make up for that inability to retain information by recording or noting everything down. Sometimes I still think that I will surely remember things, since I often forget the impairment itself, and then I am surprised when my memory fails me.

It is hard to be aware of memory problems, because you "forget that you forget things" and so it is more complicated to implement effective compensation strategies.

I also realise that there are things I won't be able to learn easily, especially if I have no prior knowledge of the subject or if they require significant organisational skills. This happened with a homeworking job that my friend offered me, with the kind intention of helping me recover some basic skills, which meant that I had to acquire specific knowledge of ICT (information and communications technology). Although I was keen to help her out and to feel useful, I realised, from my experience over the last few years, that gaining this kind of technological knowledge and managing it confidently was not within my reach at that time, and no matter how hard I tried, things would just end up confused and that wouldn't help. I think my dose of realism was essential, despite the fact that, at first, I found it difficult to accept and my friend found it difficult to understand.

Following brain injury, it is always helpful to base new learning on the person's existing knowledge. This way it is easier to codify the information in relation to something they already know, and consequently to store and recover it.

Obviously my age is a factor in my slow learning speed; however, I realise that thanks to rehabilitation and continuous brain stimulation, I now find learning easier than I did eight or ten years ago. I also know that normal people my age have no problem retaining information.

Not learning from experience, nor remembering it

When I returned home, after spending four months between hospitals and my parents' house, I was surprised to see my clothes and my things and not feel any familiarity with them, unable to remember how long I'd had a particular item of clothing or necklace, who had bought or given me something, or where it came from. This made me feel very strange, and made me realise that something wasn't working. The book *Over My Head: A Doctor's Own Story of Head Injury from the Inside Looking Out* begins with a text by the author describing this strange sensation in a similar way (Osborn, 2000). Talking about this problem later with some friends, we all came to the conclusion that, with our clothes, our things, there is an affective memory that, in me, had disappeared.

> *Difficulties recovering facts from before the brain injury are normally related to an alteration in strategies for recovering information, more than the fact that this data has been lost. The information is usually there, but the person doesn't know where to look for it.*

Nowadays I get the feeling that my CV is no use at all. I don't just mean my training, my university degrees, my years as a psychology resident or my work experience. I mean a day-to-day CV, of learning and life experience. I realise that, in recent years, I haven't been able to learn from the experience of everyday situations; it's as though my "experiential memory" is failing me.

Every day I lose my glasses, my keys or my phone. They always turn up in the end, after I've spent minutes, hours or days searching, something that never used to happen to me before, and which isn't normal in people of my age. Sometimes they appear in different places, but very often they will turn up in the same spot. During my anxious searches, these places never occur to me, and I wonder why I don't learn from the experience.

When I'm calm and everything is over (a drama with the children, a period of sleeping badly or painful sciatica, an argument with someone, etc.) I remember that this has happened before. Nacho helps me a lot by telling me so. Afterwards, writing or talking to a friend, bit by bit I can remember similar situations, how they went and how they were resolved. My problem is not being able to access all this information at the time – that would help me and relax my anxiety. What I have been able to start doing this year, at the start of one of these crisis situations, is to remember that normally I get very upset and manage to resolve things in the end. That way I can avoid the alarming sensation of this being the first time I've been in that situation, and not knowing how to resolve it.

Following brain injury, there can appear to be changes to the executive component that brings "to the fore" relevant information to unravel a given situation. This component involves many cognitive resources, since after analysing the situation we have to check through our long-term information storage for facts, events or knowledge that are of importance and activate them mentally. Again, the limitation of resources for processing information, implicit in brain injury, is behind the inability to benefit from past experiences.

Also in the last few years, especially when I've wanted to remember particular psychotherapy techniques, I have realised that I have difficulty with what I call "memory for processes". It relates to a problem with trying to remember the methodology for doing a task. There are many things I know about, but I can't teach someone else, I'm not able to transmit my own knowledge.

Very often, a person with brain injury can know that they do something, but not how they do it, which means they have automated the process and they are unable to move consciously through the steps or strategies to complete the task, which is certainly also due to limited processing resources or ineffective management of these resources. This way, the majority of processing resources (the computer's memory) are assigned to implementing the process but no part is left for "monitoring" the process consciously.

I think that my main difficulty with returning to work as an analytical psychotherapist is due to the fact that I am not aware of the steps or processes, and as I can't explain them, I feel like I can't remember them. Of course, I would be able to make a psychotherapeutic intervention automatically or guided by my intuition – my friends often tell me that I come up with the right comment or advice – but it makes me very insecure not knowing how I do it. I feel like a first year student asking my university colleagues which steps come first.

The same thing happens with English. I know what an expression or a word means, but I can't explain why. It's as though there's a fog over the tree of decisions that leads me to a result: I know how to get to the result without being able to explain why.

Chapter 5

Cognitive symptoms related to thinking

Aurora Lassaletta and Amor Bize

Difficulty summarising

I find it difficult to summarise what I want to say and express it in a concise, accurate way. Even now that I am much better, I have to make a huge effort when I speak to get to the point or say my piece in a few words. I am starting to recognise my tendency towards vague communication. Sometimes I realise that the people closest to me, who know about this difficulty, will avoid speaking to me on the phone if they are in a rush, and send SMS or WhatsApp messages instead. My brothers are experts in avoiding my lengthy digressions!

> *Following brain injury, it is common to find that some people are unable to communicate effectively and concisely what they want to transmit. They start with an idea that then gets tangled up with additional, irrelevant details, which means that sometimes they lose the thread and don't know where they want to go with what they're saying. This is an impairment to their ability to plan the message, selecting the main and additional ideas that they want to include, and a difficulty with managing processing resources, which means they allocate resources to the action of communicating and have no resources left that can remain "active" on the mental level that guides the conversation (Christensen and Uzzell, 1999).*

I can't help going round in circles when I tell a story, or making it too long, giving unnecessary details. When I make an effort to avoid that, I stay quiet for most of the time, because once I start talking it's very difficult to be specific. Lately it has helped me to be able to express this difficulty out loud. I have no problem doing that with someone I'm close to. With a friend, when I start talking about something, before I go on for too long, I say, "Sorry, it's really hard for me to keep things short, I'll try to get to the point. If you catch me going round in circles, just give me a nudge". And if I'm prepared for it, and I'm talking to someone alert, I'm more able to talk about just three or four key ideas without sending anyone to sleep. Another great strategy that helps me is giving just the headlines, like a newspaper, especially if I'm with people I haven't seen for a while and we have a lot to tell one another. If they then want more information about one of the headlines; well, they often have to be patient!

I'm increasingly conscious of expressing myself in this way, and I can't always find alternatives, since many moments of communication are unplanned. When communication is more formal, I think about it in advance, and often decide to write down a summary of what I'm going to say. I have the paper in front of me as a reference and sometimes I read directly from it to make myself stick to the essentials. Recently, I had a meeting with my friend who works as a coach, where she asked me to evaluate the rewarding coaching process, with which she helped me enormously. I was thinking a lot about everything I wanted to tell her and I wrote it down. When I was with her I tried to remember what I had written, but when I couldn't and I started to waffle, I was able to take out the paper and read out everything I had written, which was a lot, and she said it was very rewarding.

Another feature of this new form of communication is that I go into too much detail, sometimes about myself, my story, and often to people who don't need to hear the details of my life, just the general idea. Afterwards, when some time has passed and I realise, then I regret it. It's as though I can't set a limit once I have started the conversation. Later I get embarrassed that someone I don't know very well knows so many personal details about my life, when I might not know anything about theirs. A year ago, requesting a reduction to a course fee, filling out the "Grounds for Grant Application" section I once again gave too many details about myself, and later, when I met the tutor, I felt uncomfortable, because of the imbalance in how much personal information we knew about each other. Now, before I start to write or talk about myself, alarm bells start ringing in my head that say: "STOP! You don't need to give details", and just in case they don't start ringing, I have a post-it note with the STOP sign stuck to my computer monitor.

I have identified with Sheena McDonald, when her husband Allan explains in their book *Rebuilding Life After a Brain Injury* how she would tell all her personal week schedule to a plumber on the phone when she was trying to find a suitable time for him to come to fix something (McDonald, Little and Robinson, 2019).

> *When performing any activity, like a discussion, people often spontaneously monitor it, so that they can make any necessary changes or corrections as they go along. However, following brain injury, processing resources are not managed efficiently, or are so limited that they can't be used on both tasks at once: either you are saying what you want to transmit, or you are monitoring whether what you are saying matches what you want to say or had thought of sharing. This means it is common to review (if you do) only after you've finished speaking or doing whatever it was, which reduces the room for manoeuvre and the sensation of self-efficacy.*

I am increasingly aware that often I don't distinguish priorities from non-essential things, not only when choosing what I talk about, but in many other situations. In my daily targets for rehabilitation and completing everyday activities, this impairment can have significant consequences if I am not alert. At the beginning of my rehabilitation, I started to worry and get angry because I thought there were no employment options for people in my situation, and I even wanted to raise the issue with lawyers. Luckily, Nacho helped me to see that at that time all my energy had to be focused on my physical and cognitive recovery, without using up my time and effort on anything else.

In daily life, I sometimes get fixated on a tiny, incidental thing that one of my sons has done, and I can't judge it with perspective until I stop and breathe calmly and figure out whether it is essential or not, or they point it out to me themselves.

When I get home after a conversation with my brothers or my friends, I realise that during the time we were socialising I focused on something entirely secondary, and didn't talk about anything that is important to me or the other person.

At the beginning of my third year of working on this book, I became very aware of this limitation. I had a lot written; in fact for the last year and a half all I did was gather huge quantities of material that I had written over the past five years. When I came to decide how to name, collate and organise it, I often couldn't distinguish the priority material from the secondary. Later, with everything in front of me, grouped in blocks, after going through it once summarizing and editing, with help, it was hard to start out on the second pass. I had "everything" in front of me and it was difficult to focus on just one of the parts. Suddenly I was struggling to make decisions and prioritise, and again I had to ask for guidance, to see what the order of the steps should be. I used to be quite independent in my work, but I can see that I'm gradually accepting the current reality of my dependence in certain tasks.

Concrete thinking

These days, I really struggle to understand abstract and philosophical words. My friend, who is a professional coach, can vouch for that. In the personal coaching that I did with her, I always asked her to explain exactly what certain words meant. Although I understood them, I couldn't grasp their deeper meaning: "challenges", "processes", "legacy". I called them the "big words". I understand things better if the language is specific, and that was not the case before. I can see this when I read through some of my old clinical sessions presented in my work. To get back into reading, I made a wise choice, in this sense, in reading the whole *Harry Potter* collection. I no longer see myself enjoying Oscar Wilde's deft double-entendres the way I used to. The first time I went back to a conference, in 2018, I mentioned this residual problem to one of the professionals and I was very surprised to learn that it was a common symptom, something he had written about himself, and which I later read (Salas, Vaughan, Shanker and Turnbull, 2013). He was also surprised, because it was the first time he had heard a patient identify this impairment.

> *Following brain injury, it is common to find that the person has lost abstract thought and works on a more concrete or tangible level than before. As such, their language also becomes more concrete; they do not use complex terms as they used to; and they struggle to understand the meaning of such terms. Again, the consequence we see is limited processing resources, which makes it difficult to train in the "top league".*

I have also realised that the language I use is more concrete than the language I used in the past. This happens in Spanish, but also in English; I speak with a fairly basic vocabulary, nothing fancy. I'm sure that relates to the same thing. In Ireland, I attended an English course for a few days. It was very interesting; we had to come up with a short story at home, at our own speed. I was thrilled by this idea, and imagine my surprise when I read my story and realised that it could have been written by a twelve-year-old. Knowing that I didn't have many symbolic resources to add, I did manage to incorporate one of the characteristics I haven't lost: my sense of humour. That was the key to making my story original and funny, and I was very happy with it. My thinking has become much more "literal", and now I'm starting to read accounts by others who refer to the same thing (Yeoh, 2018).

To rediscover my place in the world after the physical and emotional earthquake, I felt that music might be a path and a language that would help me connect. And I found an incredible women's choir that accepted me, with my schedule and my rhythm. It wasn't just the music – it was the relationship, finding this rich and varied group of women, where I met sisters, friends, aunts, carers, directors, managers and fairy godmothers, who had a lot to teach me. Thank you, ladies, I feel so lucky to have been able to share this space with you and grow together! I love the democratic group dynamic of the choir. I find it very interesting to listen to these women. One of them, a professor of employment law and now a friend, talks and writes very well. She has given me several of her articles and, when I read them, I feel like a child who can't keep up, because the concepts are so abstract. The same thing happens when I listen to her talk at choir about something profound. I have to switch off because I can't understand or follow the conversation, which is full of metaphors and philosophical ideas. This never used to happen to me before, when I was able to understand and prepare lectures and papers with abstract and symbolic content for my work.

> *It is common for people who have suffered brain injury to report difficulties with understanding a text, which means that they read the same paragraph several times until they have fully understood the idea. Sometimes, they summarise or underline the most important words to facilitate the task of getting to the crux of the matter.*

I remember how hard it was, and still is, to understand particular books and films. In addition to the attention problems and fatigue, there is also this problem with understanding whenever the film is particularly symbolic, like *Three Colours: Blue* by Krzysztof Kiéslowski. However, I am very pleased to see that my understanding of films is improving. That brings to mind *The King's Speech*, and how difficult I found it to understand. Several years later, I watched the film again, and it seemed much more straightforward.

My thinking is also now more concrete; it is as though I can't see beyond what I have in front of me. It feels as though someone has put blinkers on me, like they do with donkeys, which sometimes stops me thinking with perspective. This morning, I had to drive my son to a place where we had agreed to meet another mother who would take all the children to their final destination, to save everyone making the longer journey. We were running late. I sent messages to the mother to let her know, and I felt awful because we were keeping several people waiting. When I had finally dropped off my son, and apologised profusely, I got to thinking, angry with myself: how had it not occurred to me to tell the mother that I was grateful for her offer, but because we were running late, I would take Álvaro straight to the final destination myself, and stop everyone else having to wait for me? I was annoyed that this only occurred to me afterwards. There are a lot of these occasions, when I think that I must seem awful to the other person, who doesn't know how limited my brain is when it comes to thinking with perspective. But neither do I!

> *In this case, we find it difficult to deviate from the original script if there is a setback ("being late"). Since all your processing resources are dedicated to this plan of action (and in an anxious situation processing resources are reduced even further), you cannot assess in situ an alternative plan to implement.*

The other day, when I went to collect the car to go to my choir rehearsal, I met a good friend outside my house. We started talking when, suddenly, there was a cold breeze that we weren't dressed for, so we decided to finish the conversation and go on our way. She was even less wrapped up than I was, and her house is around a ten-minute walk away. At that point it didn't occur to me to offer her a lift home that would only take a second. Later, when I thought about it, I couldn't believe that I wasn't able to think with more perspective at the time.

> *It is very complicated for anything that is not explicit or programmed to occur spontaneously to a person who has suffered brain injury. The capacity to improvise, deviate from the plan, generate alternatives to what had originally been thought of, requires very many processing resources, which are even more limited following a brain injury.*

Now, fourteen years after my head trauma, I have also been able to read a few professional books, more slowly and with greater attention, such as *Neuropsychological Rehabilitation* (Muñoz Céspedes and Tirapu, 2001), which was recommended to me at the end of my rehabilitation treatment in 2007. I asked for books that could help me to understand what was happening to me, and I still find them difficult to read. All these years later, I still have difficulty understanding the theoretical side if it's not backed up by practical examples.

Chapter 6

Cognitive symptoms related to lack of awareness

Aurora Lassaletta and Amor Bize

Lack of awareness of the real situation

When I came out of the coma after my accident, of course I wasn't really aware of what had happened to me. In the times when I wasn't asleep, I was quite animated and I wasn't aware of the damage I had suffered or its consequences. I remember a hospital visit from my boss at the mental health centre when I asked him to just rearrange my patients for a couple of weeks, because then I would be back at work. I was saying that as I managed to sit up for the first time, after a month of absolute rest. It was another three months before I started walking.

> *In the initial period following a brain injury, in the acute stage of hospitalisation, people can often suffer 'anosognosia', which means they lack the awareness to realise the extent of the impairments they are suffering. To be aware of the real situation they are in, they require sufficient cognitive resources to analyse the situation overall and these people tend to "function automatically", with the image of themselves that they had before the injury (Wilson, Herbert and Shiel, 2003).*

The issue of my lack of awareness makes me think about my aunt, to whom I am very close, when she came to visit me in hospital, and her emotional tears when she saw that I was critical but alive. I didn't understand anything in that moment – I wondered why she was crying, I couldn't understand how she was feeling – but years later I can recognise it and am grateful for her sincerity. I understand that everyone does their best when they visit a critically ill person in hospital, myself included, but I honestly believe that hers was the most genuine visit I received. After many visitors who told me how well I looked, she gave me a hint of the shock that was in store for me later, when I first made it to the bathroom mirror in my wheelchair and came face to face with my new appearance.

As a clinical psychologist, I also interpret this initial lack of awareness as a necessary defence mechanism for overcoming the first stage of physical recuperation, keeping up the person's spirits and energy to tolerate the initial rest phase and the arduous rehabilitation of fractures and wounds. Later, my awareness also returned gradually. When I did recover movements and the ability to stand, I very slowly started to register my cognitive impairments, my difficulty processing information, my fatigue and many other consequential symptoms.

> *On the other hand, becoming aware of physical impairments is faster and easier because they are tangible, visible problems that are apparent even within the limited scope of actions required in a hospital. Cognitive impairments, however, require a person to face tasks that pose a challenge or call for more cognitive resources than are normally used by a hospital patient. The person also needs to remember situations in which they have recently failed, because when memory is altered, the person can only remember how they would have handled the situation before the injury and does not implement strategies to compensate for their current impairments.*

This lack of awareness, although it helped me to move forward, to have the strength to face different rehabilitation programmes, also caused me problems. My conviction and comments about going straight back to work made one colleague make work-related decisions that she later regretted, and she was angry with me.

I remember how at the Base Centre where they confirmed my disabled status, I rejected the percentage they had given me, saying that I didn't want to "sponge off the state". They explained to me that the percentage was calculated according to the chronic nature of some of my symptoms and that I would come to understand. I also requested an extraordinary appointment with the Medical Board to ask whether, dismissing the medical reports, they could cancel my incapacity for work. They told me that normally people ask to increase their disability level, not reduce it, and that, although I wasn't aware of it at the time, the disability level made sense for me.

Gradually, I became aware of the side effects and impairments resulting from the accident, and now I realise that, from the outside, they had calculated perfectly the extent of the effects that would impact on various situations in my day-to-day life. After a lot of external and internal work, I have also learned to calculate it.

Although many people around me are more aware of what is happening to me than before, I don't know to what extent. At first, my father, with the best of intentions, was preoccupied by my work prospects and was job-hunting for me. I never tired of telling him that I loved my job and that if the professionals and I could see that I was in a condition to work I could certainly get my place back as a clinical psychologist – a job I was passionate about, and for which I had done all the work to achieve my specialty in Clinical Psychology (PsyD) and to complete training in other areas.

> *Sometimes, it is also hard for the family of the person with brain injury to recognise the cognitive impairments they are suffering, because there is still no information on how they would handle a situation at work, for example. It is normal for people to tell professionals that their relative's memory is fine because they can perfectly remember holidays from five years ago, but they don't realise that they are unable to learn the name of the physiotherapist working with them on a daily basis, or how to get from their room to the hospital gym.*

At the moment, I feel a strange mixture of excess awareness of many things and a lack of awareness of others, which I don't understand very well. On the one hand, I have extra analysis, particularly self-analysis of my behaviour and movement, which often prevents me from relaxing or switching off. According to the neuropsychologist, this is related to an exacerbation of a very analytical personality trait. Then again, for other things, I still show a lack of awareness, not accepting my limitations and setting myself unrealistic targets.

I struggle to recognise how slow and difficult certain changes can be. I get too excited about things at first, no doubt because of my personality, and I should be more realistic. Whenever I have started any kind of rehabilitation, I have come out of the first appointment feeling very excited, believing that my symptoms would improve considerably and quickly with this treatment. After a while, there would be the comedown, the realisation that changes are very slow and very small, or even that there would be no change in some of the symptoms. Nacho was always by my side, with a more realistic outlook; at first, I got angry with him, called him a pessimist and shouted at him for not believing in me. After a while, I think that his dose of realism did me good, but without my rebelliousness, and the desire to recover, I could not have made any progress. If we combine our characteristics, realism and rebellion, we make a great team!

> *Good executive functioning is essential in making a suitable assessment of possible success or failure in a specific situation, because it requires all these aspects to be integrated simultaneously at a given moment:*
>
> - *Making an overall assessment of the situation: what does this situation require?*
> - *Knowing one's own abilities and limitations.*
> - *Comparing the requirements of the situation with one's own capacities and assessing the outcome.*
> - *In the case of a negative outcome, assessing whether any aspect of the situation can be changed to give a favourable outcome: adapting the situation to one's own abilities (Wilson, 2003).*

My lack of awareness also helped me to face and get back into things, like returning to training at the Gestalt school where I had been studying. Even I am impressed with the way I overcame the fatigue to listen and participate, semi-reclined, in the workshops and sessions. It's true that there was little theory and it was very much experience-based, and that really suited me, even though I still didn't have much emotional connection.

The work I do to avoid this lack of awareness is to set myself some realistic goals for each season (which makes me sound like a professional sportsperson!). Calmly, and asking the opinion of the people closest to me who know how I am, I can set myself some real goals with awareness. There are many times when I get carried away and my head starts to connect images like in the tale of "The Milkmaid and Her Pail", I see myself as the mother of a very large family, going back to work, taking long trips to the mountains, cooking for big events . . . it's great for motivation, but I have to put the brakes on immediately so that accepting my impairments does not become too painful, and I can keep on enjoying what I have already achieved.

I am increasingly aware of the repercussions and consequences of my side effects on the people I love and live with. I am now also able recognise many phases of considerable lack of empathy on my part, which I now regret. Knowing that this is a common symptom after an ABI, as I read in Tim's story, has helped me to be kinder to myself and to find ways of compensating (Wilson, Winegardner and Ashworth, 2014).

I think it is very important to give information about the most frequent symptoms in an ABI, and especially about the invisible symptoms, in the therapy groups I coordinate. Simply explaining that lack of awareness of their deficits is a very common symptom in people with ABI is already helping to generate knowledge and awareness. I have read that some rehabilitation centres – such as the Oliver Zangwill Centre for Neuropsychological Rehabilitation in Ely, UK – offer, as a fundamental part of integrative treatment and to reduce anosognosia, psychoeducational workshops that explain how the brain, and brain damage, works, and where participants even learn to read brain scans (MRIs). The effectiveness of treatment at this centre for people whose brain injuries occurred many years before their treatment strengthens my hopes for continuing my recuperation and rehabilitation. I was moved to read about the personalised tool that Robert, a patient, created there, during his rehabilitation, to broaden his awareness and that of those around him. He made a card with a picture of his brain scan and a list of his major residual disabilities on the back. He shows it whenever he meets someone new, or reads it when he gets into difficult situations. As Robert says, it is very liberating to find out the causes of your problems, even though it won't solve them (Wilson, Winegardner and Ashworth, 2014).

After so many years of living with disabilities resulting from ABI, I feel that using a tool like a video recording of myself would have helped me a lot in earlier years, both to assess my development and to increase awareness of my deficits. I would encourage other people affected to record themselves from time to time – even better if they can get someone to help with the filming and if they can answer the same questions. Watching them back after some time helps to assess the development of various functions from a starting point. Any tools we can invent, like Robert did, to help broaden our awareness and the awareness of those around us are very useful. Some professionals, like C. Keohane and L. Prince, use "video feedback" as a communication tool (Winson, Wilson and Bateman, 2017).

Part 3

Behavioural, emotional and physical symptoms

Chapter 7

Behavioural symptoms

Aurora Lassaletta and Amor Bize

Impulsivity and verbal incontinence

All too often I just can't stop myself from speaking. My impulsivity makes me say things I shouldn't and don't want to say, even though I'm thinking them. I've lost count of the number times I've said things I immediately regret, to those close to me – who are getting used to it – and to other people, with whom I really would prefer to keep quiet. It's as though, because of this impulsivity, my social skills have regressed. I'm very conscious of this change. I've always been a very thoughtful person, and I used to enjoy going unnoticed. Now, I sometimes find myself in conflict situations that I don't know how to handle and I barely recognise myself.

> *Following brain injury, particularly if it affects executive functions (linked to the frontal lobe), it is common to experience difficulty with reflecting carefully before saying or doing things. Loved ones often say that they find that the person with brain injury is "more direct" or they now "call a spade a spade", and this often causes conflict in personal relationships. This happens because the person with brain injury does not stop to think about the consequences of what they want to do or say; they also have difficulty putting themselves in the position of the person hearing their comments and, if they do, it's often too late (Prigatano, 1999).*

Saying everything I think as a mother, partner, daughter, daughter-in-law, sister-in-law, etc., is not always appropriate, especially when I'm being negative. I have always been quite sarcastic, but I would normally realise whether a comment was fitting or not. Now I've lost that gauge and sometimes I come out with things out of context, or when it would be better not to say anything at all, such as during meetings, or family dinners.

Years later, now that I have started to read the stories of other people affected, I realise that this residual disability is very common in us, and we constantly feel the need to apologise for our verbal impulsivity, as Alex explains in his account (Wilson, Winegardner and Ashworth, 2014).

It is estimated that impulsivity affects 70 per cent of people who have suffered head trauma. Verbal impulsivity manifests in making inappropriate (sometimes offensive) comments, giving the first answer that comes to mind when asked a particular question, verbose discourse and difficulty letting the other person speak. This type of behaviour sometimes makes it difficult to normalise social interactions.

I also tend to interrupt people while they are talking to me. Sometimes it's an impulse, sometimes it's because I'm afraid that if I wait I will forget what I want to say. Luckily, when I realise what the problem is, I can explain: "Sorry for interrupting, but I don't want to forget to tell you this". It may be that just a quick introduction is enough to be able to carry on talking about it later, when it's my turn.

I notice myself being impulsive even in my quiet moments, playing word games on my tablet. One of the friends I regularly play with will often make long words using all the letters, which give her lots of points. She almost always beats me. Whereas when I see a possible play, I do it immediately, even if it's only a few letters; I write the first word that comes into my head. I can't overcome the impulse, reflect and see whether I could score more points by making a word with all the letters.

Impulsivity can be related to difficulty in regulating your own emotions, controlling impulses and desires in the moment and demonstrating social conduct that is appropriate in each situation (impairment to the ventromedial prefrontal cortex). It can also be related to problems with focusing attention properly, suppressing distractions or habitual answers, or planning to reach a goal (injury to the ventrolateral prefrontal cortex).

I once heard the psychologist from CEADAC talking about impulsivity and linking this feature of the person's current personality to their brain injury. He told me that taking this impulsivity into account would help him to set physiotherapy targets. I was very keen to meet physiotherapists who understood brain injury and worked like this, and he put me in touch with someone who enabled me to understand my symptoms much better and not psychologise everything that was happening to me.

I think that due to my insecurity, or not being able to control everything that is happening to me, I am generally more irritable, and sometimes I will have an emotional outburst without any warning. When situations are emotionally charged I hit my limit straight away, I have much less patience and I lose my temper impulsively – I can't control it. These new aspects that affect temperament are difficult to manage (Wilson, Winegardner and Ashworth, 2014) and should also be addressed in treatment.

Tendency to passivity

I tend to be as passive and still as possible, if it's left up to me. Recently, I asked my older brother if I had always been like that, and he told me that I was not like that at all before the accident. He described me as a very active person, who found it difficult not to have plans and to stay still for very long. I always found an excuse to get out of the house.

These days, I feel that I'm constantly fighting my natural rhythm, my tendency to passivity. By nature, I want to be calm, passive, not to move around or be too active. I really lack the initiative to start moving. I feel like I have no internal engine; the engine has to come from outside, with timetables and commitments. I stop doing many things because I don't have the drive, and then I feel terrible about not making the most of my time.

> *After brain injury, people may tend to inactivity due to alterations in motivation and initiation components that are dependent on executive functions. On the other hand, as we have already mentioned, the reduction in processing resources means that each activity demands a considerably greater effort, and the person tends to economise those resources.*

This passivity is above all physical, unless there is significant cognitive fatigue. My mind is normally quite active, and actually engages in a lot of over-analysis. When I'm exhausted, or there are too many visual or cognitive stimuli, there is also mental passivity, but I would call this a defence mechanism, or withdrawal due to saturation.

I thought that my passivity was something to do with physical tiredness, and it's true that it gets worse if I'm tired, but I can tell that it is not caused by exhaustion. When I'm left alone, and I'm not tired and I can choose what to do, I often still tend to be passive and quiet.

A tendency to passivity is known as apathy, and can appear with varying levels of severity. If it is very severe, the person might stay sitting on the sofa "watching" television for hours and hours, without demanding any other activity, not even going to the toilet, or drinking water, for example. This is related to a difficulty with setting goals and proposing activities, even if they would be very enjoyable for the person.

It seems like I'm lethargic, like I don't want to do anything. Often, from the outside, people have interpreted this trait as a mood disorder, but it really has to do with something neurological. I know I don't have low mood, but I do get overwhelmed by apathy.

It is very important to make a differential diagnosis with a depressive disorder, since the two things are very commonly confused. Passivity after brain injury can be related to executive functions (motivation, initiation, engagement) and related to the frontal lobe, and it is different from a mood disorder. In fact, often the person with brain injury does not experience any feeling of sadness, loss of appetite or sleep problems.

I also very often find myself wandering aimlessly. Sometimes I stop in the middle of a movement, and don't continue it. This is also related to memory, because maybe I forget where I was going, or what I was going to do, but I think that, to some extent, that happens to everyone. The delay in movement is sometimes due to an order from the brain that doesn't arrive, but not always. Sometimes I might stand staring at my breakfast mug and people around me will say, "Wake up, get a move on, please!" My family sometimes affectionately mimic me, just standing in the middle of the room, hands on hips. One day we saw a TV report, filmed at CEADAC, which mentioned this loss of drive as a symptom of brain injury. When we heard that, we started to understand and accept it a little more.

Just as the initiation of a given activity may be altered, we can also find it difficult to sustain an action until we reach the proposed goal. This could be due to a failure to stay focused on the action itself, and as a consequence the affected person jumps to another internal stimulus (thought, emotion) or external stimulus (person speaking, television), neglecting what they were doing. On other occasions, it is the appearance of something new or unexpected that challenges the automatic way of carrying out the action and demands an adjustment that the affected person can no longer carry out so immediately.

To compensate for this passive tendency I have had to structure my time with a timetable, as if I were back at school. Otherwise, I can spend two hours or more without doing anything, just staring into space.

To help me create a more dynamic routine, I have introduced commitments into my day-to-day life that, specifically because they are commitments, have helped me to combat my tendency to passivity. For example, I start the day with the task of taking my children to school. This is a commitment, since they can't be late, so I do it on time. This means that I recharge my batteries to get up early, wake them up, make breakfast, and then make sure they pack their school bags, brush their teeth and get to school on time, almost always. First obstacle of the day, overcome!

Thanks to what I've learned through my different rehabilitation processes, I have decided to take on certain responsibilities that help me to break with passivity, and this is crucial for me and my family. Besides going back and forth to school, I do the shopping, some days I cook, I play sports at set times on set days, I go to choir and I'm writing my book! This way, I have a routine that gets me out of that tendency a little bit, but without going too far for my current condition, which, in reality, is more passive than before.

Implementing routines that plan daily activities is the most effective way to overcome the apathy or inactivity of people with brain injury, although it is necessary to respect moments of rest and to not generate excessive demands that lead to situations of frustration or significant fatigability (Wilson, 2003).

I used to be very hard on myself, thinking I was lazy, idle, attributing my passivity and negligence to a lack of interest. I imagine that if I had physical injuries or more severe brain injury, we would have been more able – both myself and those around me – to accept this impairment, but being physically much better I find it difficult to accept this tendency to do nothing, not to move, not to think, not to want to register visual or cognitive stimuli.

Very often, relatives of a person with brain injury report that they have become idle or lazy, and this interpretation of their family member's behaviour causes a lot of conflict at home and a feeling of guilt in the person affected. Knowing that this is another consequence of brain injury helps to normalise the situation, and to address it as another rehabilitation goal that does not just depend on the person's will to recover.

Doctors stress the need for physical exercise, and I make a real effort to stick to that rule and move around, take walks. I have even lost the drive to chase after the ball in paddle tennis. The effort it takes for me to do sports is huge, especially if you take into account this tendency to passivity, and the fear of "neurological fatigue". Unless my physical complaints are flaring up, planning some sporting activity and completing it every week with a specific timetable helps me to get my exercise without dwelling on it too much, and to feel better.

At first, I was barely interested in anything. Now I'm regaining my interest in activities I like, but sometimes my tendency to do nothing takes over and I might back out of a plan, or cancel it, especially if I'm very tired.

When my husband and children are out and I have a day "to myself", I stick to my true rhythm, two miles per hour. I can't help it. That's just what happens, even when I'm not particularly tired. And it's better that I accept it. I don't know how to manage or enjoy my free time, unless it's scheduled. I have always really enjoyed watching a film, reading a book, being with friends, going to an exhibition or even chatting on the telephone, and I still enjoy doing those things; but nowadays the initiative almost never comes from me when I have a free moment. The suggestion almost always has to come from somebody else. If I just let myself go with the flow, what my body – and often my mind – wants is total passivity.

Although it might sound strange, I give myself the task of watching a TV series methodically, because at night, when my children have gone to bed, left to my own devices I wouldn't do anything, not even turn on the TV. Getting back to reading has been wonderful, and when I get hooked on a book it's hard to put it down; I can even lose hours of sleep. I absolutely agree with Christopher Yeoh, who was affected, like me, by an ABI following a head trauma, and who considers reading an escape and refuge when things aren't working out (Yeoh, 2018). Yet, however much I love reading, sometimes I don't even have the urge to pick up a book that's sitting beside me.

They do say that without passivity there is no creativity, and I think that's true, but I would really like passivity to be a choice.

Sometimes I feel like my body doesn't want to start any action at all, as if it doesn't have much life in it, and it prefers a state of minimal energy expenditure. It's as if it's lost all its passion.

After brain injury, it is common to observe an absence or significant reduction in sexual desire in people who previously enjoyed their sexuality. This change is related to anhedonia – a loss of interest or satisfaction in activities that the person previously found pleasurable – and usually occurs in people whose brain injury affects the frontal lobes. On the other hand, there are also people with an injury to the front of the brain who present with sexual disinhibition, in the same way that they demonstrate impulsivity or increased psychomotor agitation.

I loved my work as a clinical psychologist, and I love giving the Accepting Your Impairments workshops that I sometimes coordinate as a volunteer. Being able to lead those workshops gives me back part of my professional identity; it allows me to share and to help participants to express how they feel about their progress and their impairments. I feel good and I'm very happy with the positive evaluations I get at the end of the workshop.

At first, I always had the idea that I wanted to take another workshop next term, but then I didn't call, I didn't organise it, the term went by and often they had to call me from the centre to ask when I was going to start, to give me a nudge, and then I would go. Of course, I know that a one-hour workshop each week is an intense activity that will mean I can't do any other activities that day, and I don't plan any other activities like this in the same period. This is something I am motivated to do, but the drive is still not there.

An essential tool for improving this loss of drive and the tendency to passivity, once again, is being aware of it and accepting it. Even now, I am still a little unaware and ignore it. It makes me laugh just thinking about it, but sometimes I really do believe that I will wake up in the morning and be the person I used to be. It's as if there's a huge difference that could be reconciled by synchronising my internal mental experience and my external bodily experience.

I understand that not getting on the exercise bike, not being active or not reaching goals that you set yourself to lead a healthier life happens to everyone, because we don't have time between work, family, etc. However, in reality, I don't work and my goal is to dedicate my time to the best possible physical and cognitive rehabilitation, and I still can't do it.

I loved the recommendation of finding an exercise buddy, a friend to make plans with, someone who is counting on you and waiting for you (Denton, 2008), which makes sure you show up.

I now realise that, if I want to do physical activity as rehabilitation, I have to include it in my weekly timetable in a structured way. Even so, there is no guarantee I will do it. I sometimes think that if I won the lottery I would hire someone to work as my external motivation. They would have to pick me up at my house and take me to sports activities. I have no major difficulties with external mobility but I do have problems when it comes to my internal mobility.

Thanks to this new capacity for stillness, I am now the perfect patient for MRI scans, and a perfect target for being buried in the sand by kids. I have also been congratulated on my immobility during an acupuncture session.

I also think that I could work as an actress, presenting some of the effects of brain injury, because it would not be acting, it would be the expression of my actual impairments, which, with effort, I can maximise or minimise.

Loss of improvisation

Alongside my difficulty to adapt to changes, I also lost the ability to improvise – one of the skills I used to have, and which I miss the most. Before, on days when I had a late shift at work, if I hadn't had time to prepare food in advance, I would use my imagination and find a solution within fifteen minutes to turn four ingredients into a fairly tasty and nutritious meal. I could also improvise arrangements quickly and efficiently, at the last minute. I even got out of a hefty fine many years ago, thanks to my improvisation skills!

Now I have lost most of that wonderful ability. For a while, I had a difficult time because I believed that I still had it, and I would get anxious in those extreme situations that I was used to resolving at the last minute by improvising, which I now cannot resolve at all.

> *Adapting to changes is actually very closely related to improvising, because it requires a departure from routine, from established protocol, and proposing a new way of doing things. Improvising also has the added complication that there is no possibility of preparing for the change; it must be done on the spur of the moment, which means that the consumption of processing resources is even greater.*

However, I am very happy to see myself developing, pleased to be recovering something of my lost improvisation skills. This happens, above all, at the weekend, or at times of relaxation. If I have to stick to timetables or schedules, improvisation gets blocked.

One of my greatest passions was, and still is, travelling. I have always loved planning trips, and I think I'm pretty good at it. I learned from my mother, who is a master of the art. Now I can enjoy this ability, as long as I take into account what I have to do far enough in advance, and at my own speed, taking breaks. I couldn't do it in a short time or under pressure like before, but with time and carefully organised information, in the end I can put the pieces of the puzzle together and that gives me great satisfaction.

Decisions about what to visit when, and drawing up a hypothetical schedule, are much easier at a distance than in the moment. I need to come up with a definite plan, because now I can't improvise on the go if I don't have a schedule. It's as though I could organise things, if I had plenty of time, for a pre-recording, but I couldn't do a live broadcast. The times that I have had to make an impromptu decision have been very difficult. By contrast, I remember an Interrail journey that I took with friends many years ago, which was entirely based around improvisation. I couldn't take a trip like that now, but as the song goes, "they can't take that away from me"!

> *Improvising means arranging a new plan of action when we are already in the situation that calls for it, so it requires considerably more cognitive resources than calmly planning outside the situation itself, without the stress of urgency.*

At the moment, the important work of being conscious of how I am means that I try to avoid extreme situations and, if they do arise, now that I'm hardly the queen of improvisation, to accept it.

Chapter 8

Emotional symptoms

Aurora Lassaletta and Amor Bize

Affective flattening and emotional inexpressiveness

Emotional disconnection is another side effect that I have been discovering over the years, and, I think, recovering from to some extent.

I have been told that in the first few months I suffered a kind of affective anaesthesia. This surprised those around me, because before the accident I was quite an expressive and affectionate person. After the accident, I seemed indifferent, apathetic and distant compared to how people were used to seeing me. It was difficult for me to understand my children's emotions, let alone those of other adults. I struggled to put myself in their shoes. It was a period when noise bothered me and I needed a long time to adapt to every situation. Gradually, and with a lot of psychotherapy and neurofunctional work, I have begun to feel emotions again, perhaps with less intensity, but at least I can feel them. It still takes a lot of effort to manage and handle my feelings. When I am tired or overwhelmed, certain emotions, like anger, sometimes explode out of proportion, whereas others, like happiness and even fear, struggle to come out. I used to be very skittish, and surprise myself by making a lot of fuss. Now I feel as cold and detached as Robocop!

The difficulty with expressing my emotions was constant from the outset, and is still there, despite now being able to connect with them better. I remember how emotional I felt the first time I sang, with the choir, one of the verses of *The Cicada*, by María Elena Walsh: "Singing in the sun, like the cicada, after a year below the earth".

One New Year's Day, when I was particularly physically and mentally exhausted, even though I hadn't been out or had a drink the night before, my seven-year-old niece asked me, "Why do you seem groggy?" I asked her what she meant and, when she didn't know how to explain, I asked her to do an impression of me. She spoke like a robot, with no movement, no facial expression or gestures, and that was when I realised this aspect that I hadn't previously been aware of. Children, with their honesty and spontaneity, are my best teachers. Despite not having any significant problems with facial paralysis, I am increasingly conscious of my lack of movement, my static face.

After suffering brain injury, people can lose the richness that is conveyed by non-verbal communication: gestures, intonation, rhythm, speed of speech, etc. This means that their communication capacity is significantly limited. As such, communication can be characterised as monotonous, inexpressive or unemphatic.

Two years after my injury, I got a big surprise on an important day, when I gave an oral presentation of my thesis at the end of my postgraduate course in Gestalt therapy. The chosen topic was related to my personal story over the last few years, and I was pleased that I had been able to work into it many of the emotions and feelings I had experienced. The three-year course had been interrupted by my accident, and I was very proud of having been able to resume it after several months and complete it at the same time as my peers. It was essentially an experience-based course, nothing theoretical; because of that and the adaptations they made possible for me, I was able to continue. The disappointment came when, after my presentation, the tutor told me that my speech hadn't conveyed any emotion, that it seemed like I was merely reading aloud, that she had felt the presentation lacked all feeling, as though I were just reading from a journal. That left me confused, and made me realise that what I felt bore no relation to the way I expressed it; I couldn't show the extent of it, and at that time I was feeling a great deal. I realise that, if I had been more aware of this symptom at the time, it would have been easier to listen to her feedback. But since I wasn't, it was quite painful to hear.

Following brain injury, we can perceive changes in the capacity for transmitting the emotions that we feel, both a deficit and an excess. As such, a person can seem inexpressive despite being deeply emotional, or be in floods of tears whilst seeming only a little upset by the situation.

I am getting used to not being able to cry; even when I feel deep sadness, I can't express it. This has happened not only in the hardest times, when I lost people I was very close to, like my grandmother or much loved uncles and aunts, but also in moments of feeling excited and happy, such as the retirement party they threw for my father at the hospital where he had always worked. At one point I even pretended to cry, because I became very anxious when I tried to let out the tears I felt inside but couldn't. Now I don't do that, as I know that if someone looks me in the eye, they can tell how I really feel, even if there are no tears. That was enough when I embraced my cousins following the death of another uncle, who was not as close but was still much loved.

At choir, they tell us about the importance of being expressive when we sing. I learn a lot from watching the other singers, and I can be slightly more expressive when I try. Although I am pretending to some extent, it's not like acting, because this is an action in which I express my real feelings. Yet seeing myself in a video of a choir performance is when I most recognise my new inexpressiveness, particularly because I tend to stand next to someone who is highly expressive.

My inability to express emotion gets worse when I am more tired or nervous, but again, I would say that much like other symptoms, it depends on much more than that.

Recognising my inexpressiveness makes me aware of tense emotional situations, so that I know how to act as a consequence. In reality, this means trying to express on the outside what I'm feeling on the inside, even though I have to exaggerate it and add a more dramatic touch. I think that now, thanks to being aware and being careful not to disconnect, I no longer get as many comments about my emotional flattening. I am very surprised to find that my intuition in my self-therapy was very good, identifying symptoms by myself and implementing my own treatments. Fourteen years after my accident, I'm reading books in English that refer to tools very similar to the ones I created, tools that have a name and are included in treatment at some neuropsychological rehabilitation centres (Wilson, Winegardner and Ashworth, 2014; Winson, Wilson and Bateman, 2017).

> *Executive functions, specifically the prefrontal structures of the brain, are what permit emotional regulation, modulate the expression of emotion and allow appropriate social conduct. In TBI, damage frequently occurs to the frontal lobe and dysfunctions of this kind appear either as overexpressiveness or underexpressiveness.*

When my younger brother turned 40 and, was living thousands of kilometres away, his girlfriend had the idea of sending him a video message from all his family and friends. Sometime later, I had the chance to see the recording and I was very surprised to hear myself speak. Watching myself is when I really see the difference between what I feel on the inside and how it looks on the outside. On the video, I saw a person with some disabilities, talking slowly, with very little expression in her face or body. Yet, on the inside, I feel the same as ever and I think that I'm talking at a normal speed and that my speech is expressive.

My challenge is to exaggerate my expressiveness. While on the inside I feel like it's over the top, I have to remember that from the outside it comes across with hardly any force, even when I exaggerate.

Of course, feeling like all my roles – in my case as a woman, mother, wife and professional – had been disrupted, my self-esteem was affected most of all. People with brain injury often feel frustrated when faced with various impairments, and it is usual to have some emotional and even depressive symptoms, caused by adapting to the new situation. Overnight, you find your life and the lives of those around you have radically changed. This is what we call "adjustment disorder" in the classification of mental health disorders. These adjustment symptoms can exacerbate some of the effects of the injury, which is why it is important to take the utmost care over a differential diagnosis. While this is not easy, there are professional specialists who can distinguish them very well. Emotional support for people affected and for their families is essential throughout the rehabilitation process, with everyone working together, as the family system tends to be unsettled by the change of roles. ABI does not just affect one person: it affects a family, where it is also normal for symptoms of anxiety and depression to appear (Easton, 2016). I was particularly struck by Paloma Pastor's book *The Monsoon Years*, which covers the fight to focus attention and state funding on infant ABI in Spain. The book helps to understand the difficulty posed to the family by a sudden severe brain injury affecting a child, and how stress and adapting to a new person in the family can even lead to illness in other family members (Pastor, 2019).

I believe that brain injury stops being so invisible once you come to terms with it. Acceptance is key. So is knowledge. The guilt and insecurity that you feel about your own impairments reduce once you familiarise yourself with them, get informed about them and know that they are due to a brain injury.

Posttraumatic stress disorder is also very common in many people affected by ABI. I have had some emotionally difficult periods due to this/PTSD disorder, but my family and I could tell that these were just difficult emotional times and not the symptoms of neurological damage – although some symptoms are similar and can occur with both, such as affective anaesthesia.

I am calmer knowing that many of my impairments or symptoms have seasons, come and go or are more severe at particular times. I have periods where I am physically well, and others where I'm not so well; periods of sleeping terribly – which have nothing to do with my emotions – and others when I sleep better; periods where I eat too much – again unrelated to emotional issues; periods where I am more passive, and others where I am not so. At first – an occupational hazard – I "psychologised" everything, and thought that it was due to emotional instability. Now, with the help of excellent professionals, brain injury experts, I am more able myself to distinguish and understand what can be altered with willpower and what cannot.

> *People with brain injury are much more sensitive to any variable that can affect human beings: the weather, hormonal changes, illnesses, arguments, stress, anxiety, etc.*

I want to highlight the importance of and need to pay attention to the emotional process, both of the person affected by the ABI and of their family, from the outset. I am all too familiar with this story, with grief and acceptance as its protagonists. My experience of the emotional process and that of my family and of the people I work with who are affected by brain injury are so extensive and so intense that I could write a separate book about them.

Chapter 9

Physical symptoms

Aurora Lassaletta and Susana Pajares

Body awareness and sensitivity

When I sit down and close my eyes to do a meditation or relaxation exercise, something I try to practise as a habit, I find it very difficult to be aware of my body. This is something new for me, and of course I associate it with the brain injury. After a lot of work, I now have some feeling in the left-hand side of my body and I feel more supported on that side. It is quite a worrying sensation to have no body awareness when you have your eyes closed.

When I lie down and close my eyes, I feel like the axis of my body is twisted. I have had treatments to help me connect with my body, all incomplete. I must admit that dealing with this lack of connection is hard for me and, after a long time, when I still don't see any progress, I give up. That was the case with diafreotherapy, which is an interesting body awareness work. Before the injury, through body therapy work, I was able to connect with myself; these days the loss of sensitivity doesn't help, and the exercises are hard because, when I can't feel, they become virtual exercises, and more and more I need to base what I'm doing on something concrete.

> *There are three types of sensitivity: exteroceptive (touch, temperature, superficial and deep pain), proprioceptive and interoceptive (visceral pain, distension). With brain injury, it is common for these to be affected in isolation or jointly. Proprioceptive sensitivity gives us information about our position in space and the location of each joint or segment of the body in relation to that. A change to this kind of sensitivity means "not knowing how we are positioned or how a particular extremity is positioned". If visual function, which helps us to compensate for this deficit, is also impaired, the situation is worse.*

Over time, I have registered a loss of sensitivity in particular areas of my body. I do not feel cold or heat in some areas and I have to check that I'm always covered up, because I can find myself in some uncomfortable situations, like when my shirt rides up while I'm walking and, having no thermal sensation and not being able to feel the difference, I'll end up showing my belly to everyone without meaning to. I only realize this when someone pulls my shirt down.

Luckily, I can also talk about recovering the sensation in other parts of my body. In various rehabilitation or physiotherapy exercises I have often been asked to move my hips; I tried, but I practically couldn't do it. I criticised myself for having poor coordination and deemed myself clumsy. But, as I improved with the exercises and brain stimulation, one day I found that, all of a sudden, I could dance a bit and move my hips. Well, I'm sure it was not "all of a sudden", but that all the different work adds up to one day recovering a function or an area; nevertheless, the "click" effect was very surprising for me. All of a sudden, I could do it. As if, finally, the order from my brain was reaching my hips! And now I make the most of some very fun free moments to sway my hips to music.

My body functions like a block; when I move I do so quite robotically. Although I haven't lost mobility, my brain cannot differentiate the areas of my body very well. My job, still, fourteen years after the accident, is to discriminate between the different muscle groups with the help of physiotherapists.

I don't feel like I'm in control of my physical extremities. I'm bad at judging the distance between my body and other objects, and I often bang into things, which causes injuries. The other day, in the hospital cafeteria, I took my drink back to the table where my mum was waiting for me and banged into the column on my right, really hurting my shoulder. I wasn't distracted and I had more than enough space, but I still crashed into it; I had seen the obstacle, but I'm bad at judging the distance between my body and other objects. This can happen to anyone sometimes, but it happens to me a lot, even when I'm walking slowly. I remember asking my mother to change the handles on all the doors at her house in the mountains, because they were very angular and, since I was knocking into them on a regular basis, the bangs were leaving marks on my arm.

I often bump into people in the street, the supermarket, the metro, in situations where there is no shortage of space. I have a real problem with knowing how much space my body occupies and judging the distance between me and others. I always apologise, but people obviously don't understand, and they get quite upset, I think because I look so normal.

I also stumble a lot, more at first and now less, but it still happens. At first, both I and some of the professionals thought that this problem was due to the weakness in my legs and that I needed to strengthen my ankles by doing special exercises. Gradually, I realised that this impairment was also related to something neurological. Once, when I tripped and fell surrounded by 500 mums and dads at my children's school, frustration got the better of me and that was when I had a revelation. When I'm walking I don't look down, and that's why I trip over or bang into things (the kerb, the open door of the dishwasher, the cat . . .). It's as though I've lost the ability to look out of the corner of my eye as I walk, which is an important survival reflex, like the radar of body awareness that lets me know there is an object nearby. The problem is not my ankles, or my legs, which luckily are recovering quite a lot of strength after a lot of work and exercises; I am told that the problem is ocular dysmetria. I'm sure it is, but there is also a more internal problem with calculating distance, a problem with proprioception (Kapoor and Ciuffreda, 2002), because I even bang into things at night, in the dark, when I try to walk very short distances in familiar surroundings.

The brain normally avoids unnecessary effort. To my brain, looking without both eyes synchronised seems complicated – because of the diplopia – so it doesn't even try. When I remember, I try to compensate for its laziness by moving my whole head down to look and make sure that there is nothing in the way.

> *The effect on visual function may consist of an alteration to the field of vision or a weakness or paralysis in the extrinsic eye muscles, which handle synchronised movement of both eyes in all directions. Either of the two effects will limit the field of vision and make it difficult to determine obstacles so that we can move independently. Sometimes, this impairment can be compensated with lenses, prisms or with visual re-education therapy with an optometrist (Suter and Harvey, 2011).*

When I go swimming at the pool, I have to be careful, because my body drifts to the right. If one day I forget my glasses and have to close my eyes, I always bang into the side. I am learning to correct this, making an effort to move to the left when I swim, and then I can swim straight. If I'm conscious of this impairment and think about it, I can correct it but, if I'm going quickly or thinking about something else, it always happens.

The problem with body perception is still there. Today, I gave myself two cracks on the door as I passed it, the kind that leave bruises.

Due to my abdominal insensitivity, I realise that, when I do certain exercises that involve tension in that area, because I can't feel it, I tense and force my back to compensate, which results in injuries. Before I discovered this, I couldn't understand why the pain and cramps in my back got worse when I did gentle sports activities like Pilates, speed walking or even swimming. Now, having identified the cause of my dorsalgia (back pain), it is very important that these activities are personalised and directed by people who take into account my impairments and brain injuries.

Alongside this loss of abdominal sensitivity, I have hypersensitivity in my back, hyperesthesia, which means I feel pain whenever I rest against a hard surface, like the floor, a firm mattress or a hard chair. It seems that the hyperesthesia relates to a particular sensitivity in fractured or seriously affected areas. Before I knew about this symptom, I had to attend several physiotherapy sessions and have another scan, since the doctors couldn't explain the cause of this pain.

This new extra sensitivity means I have had to change my mattress and always take an especially soft mat to any sports or rehabilitation activities. I have it to a lesser extent in my legs, which makes it very uncomfortable to wear tight clothes. I don't let people touch these areas; I find it difficult to explain why, but I have a very strong reaction, rejecting contact in these areas that have become very sensitive since they were injured. I have found a great trick for spending the weekend away from home, whether it's at a relative or friend's house or in a hotel, which is to take with me a very thin memory foam mattress that I can place on top of any mattress.

> *With brain injury, there is often a change in sensitivity to touch, which can present as a loss of sensitivity (hypoesthesia), as excess sensitivity (hyperesthesia) or as dysaesthesia, where there is an abnormal perception of stimulus (perceiving a burning or painful sensation upon normal touch stimulus).*

Insensitivity in the abdominal area is one of the most limiting effects now that I am recovering a more-or-less normal life. My body, which also appears normal, can be fine for half-an-hour or a little longer if I'm walking, doing sport or simply standing still. However, after this time, I feel like there is no structure to sustain it, due to the insensitivity in the whole middle of my trunk, front and back. As the rehabilitation doctor explained to me, the insensitivity means that the brain does not receive all the necessary information about the position of the muscles. I am currently following a physiotherapy programme to try to strengthen my abdominal area internally and externally, and to recover some sensitivity in the process. This should prevent damage to my back, which is the part I now use when I can't make a movement with my abdomen. It has taken me and my family ten years to get this effect explained and to understand it. It is so important to believe in your intuition! As I have said, in the sports activities I used to practise, and still do, I had always calculated half-an-hour as the maximum length of time I could feel okay, but I couldn't explain why.

For some time I have been using a corset or belt that the doctor recommended when I do sport. I also use it when I have to stand up or walk around for a long time, as a way of supporting the structure of my body when my body can't support itself. I had heard a few physiotherapists say that using a corset cannot strengthen muscles but, in those particular moments, as a tool for support, I find it essential. I have to be very careful of the consequences for my back of standing still for too long, and this means I have to be sure that there will be seats at any party or meeting I'm going to, or bring along my own.

> *With brain injury, there is an overall physical deconditioning that also affects muscle tone in the trunk and limbs. In the trunk, muscle weakness in the abdominal wall and lumbar spine can manifest with pain, and specific work is required to recuperate their function to protect and stabilise the spinal column.*

Sleep disturbance and loss of satiety sensation

Because of my TBI, several physical changes have appeared that I have noticed gradually, thanks to doctors with considerable knowledge of brain injury. Sleep disorders, lack of awareness of satiety when eating and other symptoms appeared gradually, reminding me that my body had stopped, and sustained damage in some areas.

Sleep disorders were completely new for me. In the first year, I needed to sleep much more during the day and I spent very few hours awake, but when these sleeping hours reduced and my days started getting back to normal, the nights started to get difficult, mainly due to broken sleep. At first, this was attributed to depression. From my own work, I knew that anxiety and low mood can cause problems falling asleep or make people wake up very early, but I didn't know what could be causing these sleep interruptions in the middle of the night and the problem with getting back to sleep, especially since I was in my thirties. The explanation also took a long time to come, but it did alleviate the worry of not understanding this effect. The neurologist who supervised my case explained that, because of the TBI, my circadian rhythms had been deregulated, which means my sleeping and waking rhythms have changed: I get sleepier during the day and I am more awake at night. I have read interesting articles on this subject (Zuzuárregui, Bickart and Kutscher, 2018) and books where I learned that it is very common for people with ABI to find that their sleep patterns change, and that special attention must be given to this issue in their assessment and treatment (Denton, 2008; Sullivan, 2008; Wilson, Winegardner and Ashworth, 2014; Winson, Wilson and Bateman, 2017).

> *With brain injury, we can quite often see an alteration in sleep rhythms that tends to manifest as hypersomnolence (need to sleep for a greater number of hours per day), difficulty getting to sleep (conciliation insomnia) and waking frequently during the night or broken sleep. This can be explained by effects in the hypothalamus region, which is responsible for regulating circadian rhythms (the 24 hour sleep/waking cycle). A greater need for rest or astenia (fatigue) can also indicate overall physical deconditioning, which explains, together with cognitive changes and muscular paresis, that the energy expenditure required to complete our daily tasks is much greater in the case of these patients.*

For several years, I have been taking melatonin, which I was prescribed to help regulate these rhythms. Melatonin helps the process of getting to sleep and, if there is a short interruption, it also helps in getting back to sleep. The problem comes when something external wakes me up at night (needing to go to the bathroom, my son asking for water, etc.) and I also have to turn on the light; afterwards, I can't get back to sleep for over two and a half hours. As soon as my brain perceives light, it thinks it's already daytime. What's more, at these hours I am lucid, clearheaded and I can perform more complicated cognitive tasks. Indeed, some parts of this book were written in the early hours of the morning.

The first dozen times this happened to me, before I knew the cause, I also associated it with something emotional and tried all kinds of solutions. I tested out everything repeatedly: relaxation exercises, getting up and walking around, reading, meditation . . . Now that I've realised it was not due to anything emotional and accepted its real cause, it can still be annoying – especially if I have to get up early the next day – but it doesn't affect me emotionally. I try not to drink too much liquid after eight in the evening, as this reduces the likelihood of waking up at midnight; the other reasons are beyond my control. When nothing external wakes me, I sleep right through and wake up nicely relaxed.

In reality, sleeping well is not easy for me at all, as this deregulation of circadian rhythms is accompanied by hyperacousis – which exacerbates any kind of sound, even my own breathing – and the hyperesthesia in my back. But I am learning to live with these effects and I try to recover the sleep during the day if it has been a difficult night. Luckily I don't tend to have more than two bad nights in a row. The other day I was remembering my Interrail trip, when I was 21, when I spent a month sleeping in shared tents, hostel rooms with twenty other people, on trains, on the deck of a ferry, on buses, in stations, and it seemed unbelievable that I could have managed to sleep in those situations, because now I would find it impossible. I feel so lucky to have enjoyed that experience when I could.

I have also found myself, since the accident, having trouble regulating my diet. I have noticed that I eat more food and more often. At first this overconsumption was also diagnosed as a symptom of anxiety. Later, the doctors saw that the impact had affected an area of my brain specifically responsible for the sensation of satiety. This means that, when I start eating, I never get to a point where I feel full and I could keep on eating indefinitely. Sometimes I need something external, such as my belt feeling tight, to give me a sign to stop. I have also read accounts after TBI of gaining weight and changes in appetite-control mechanism, like Sheena McDonald's (McDonald, Little and Robinson, 2019).

> *The hypothalamus has a neuroendocrine system regulating hunger and satiety, which receives peripheral and central nervous system (CNS) signals to balance our consumption with our energy needs. It is very common that with brain injury this function is affected by damage to the hypothalamus itself or by the alteration of the transmission of the signal from the cortex to the hypothalamus.*

Besides sleeping, another way I have tried to compensate for fatigue is by overeating. Sometimes I get the feeling that food is the only thing that can give me long-lasting energy quickly. Later, I'll realise that I'm seeking out foods that fill me up and give me nutrients, for example a steak and tomato sandwich or a stew, not a snack or something to sate a craving. This is entirely at odds with my need to lose weight, to feel lighter, which is important to lessen the fatigue. Yet at critical moments of exhaustion, this need to consume something to give me energy is imperative and hard to ignore.

If I'm anxious or stressed, I tend to eat more. That has always been the case, but even with no stress, I still eat a lot. I have some tricks to stop myself; for example, brushing my teeth, as if I'd just finished eating, or chewing gum to prevent me from consuming anything else. My metabolism also seems to have slowed down and so, if we combine the passivity, the loss of drive, the loss of satiety sensation and my slow metabolic rate, it's easy to imagine how hard it is for me to lose weight. But I'm sticking with it and not giving up.

> *Aerobic exercise is very useful at a cardiovascular level. It increases our energy expenditure, activates our circulation and respiratory rate and uses our energy reserves deposited in accumulated fat, making it the most effective way to lose weight and increase our tolerance to physical exercise.*

Loss of balance

I have noticed some strange problems with my balance. If I go at my own pace and there are no obstacles, I can keep my balance when I'm walking and even go down stairs with no problems; however, whenever there is any interference in my path, I lose it. If I'm in a rush and there is an obstacle in my way, such as my son's backpack, even if it's far away, or people crossing me on the stairs, I wobble and get scared that I will lose my balance even more. Then I need to hold on to someone or to a handrail, or stand still. The worst thing for me is arriving home to find that people have left things in the middle of the hallway that I have to dodge (shopping bags, shoes, etc.). Even though there is space to pass, just seeing the interference puts me off balance.

Being aware of this impairment, I try to stay in control, but I get very anxious if, for example, we are walking down the street and one of my children puts his school bag on wheels in front of my feet, or if there are roadworks and I have to dodge obstacles.

Observing these balance problems led me to understand my difficulty with being at a demonstration. Finding myself in the middle of an enormous group of people can make me very unstable and uncertain, no doubt because I have no points of reference that I can grab hold of if I need to. Before, I had no problems and went to lots of different crowded events, from demonstrations to concerts in football stadiums; now I assume that I can't do it.

With regard to my recovery, I can see that now, on metro journeys, I don't always need to hold on to the belt to go up the escalator. Although the floor wobbles a little, I feel more stable and more secure, especially if I'm calm and not in a hurry.

I have discovered a trick that helps me when I have no choice but to be in the middle of a large crowd. It worked very well the day that I spent with my family at a theme park full of people. The trick is to look not at people, but at the floor, at the stable point; this helps me to keep my balance.

I would have loved to be able to use Madrid's BiciMad bicycles, because one of the activities I have been able to resume with time is cycling, and I really enjoy it. But I understand that it needs to be in the countryside, with no obstacles and plenty of space in front of me. In the streets of Madrid, I would be anxious about getting confused by the noise, lack of space and continuous interference.

I'm delighted with some aspects of my progress: a while ago, at the metro, I heard that the train was arriving at my platform, and I still had a long flight of stairs to take. A girl behind me started to run, passing by me, and I concentrated and was able to take the stairs more quickly, looking at the floor, and managed to catch the train. In the past, I really wasn't so sure that this instability had anything to do with neurology. Now I am.

> *Control of posture or balance is achieved using information obtained through three channels: vision, the inner ear and proprioception in the lower limbs. It is common in brain damage for any of these pathways to be altered or for there to be an impairment in the integration of the information they collect at the central level, which will result in a loss of balance. This can also be affected by the difficulty of paying attention to different stimuli at the same time; it is a dual effect with repercussions for postural control. (Peydro de Moya, Baydal Bertomeu and Vivas Broseta, 2005; Bensoussan, Viton, Schieppati, Collado, Milhe de Bovis, Mesure and Delarque, 2007).*

Hypersensitivity to medications

Since the TBI, all medications have made me feel bad. This never happened to me before. Now, with the exception of painkillers or anti-inflammatories, I can't take any medication, because it will either make me extremely drowsy, or cause unexpected reactions in my body. The last time I was prescribed a muscle relaxant due to a strong cramp in my back, it caused severe drowsiness and vomiting, and the relaxation of some parts of my body took almost two months to wear off completely.

A few professionals have explained that, following the TBI, some areas of my brain have remained very sensitive, which is why medication can cause major reactions.

Before the doctors identified that my impairments were related to cognitive damage, they sometimes treated slow thought, fatigue or apathy as depressive symptoms, with a minimal dose of antidepressants – a dose that I was assured would not ordinarily cause any problems. However, antidepressants had anything but the desired effect. At first, the medication significantly increased my fatigue, drowsiness, and lethargy, so I had to abandon it. These side effects of medication are entirely counterproductive in my situation, since I was looking for the exact opposite from my rehabilitation and daily efforts. Some of the effects of the damage have been improving a little with neurofunctional and neuropsychological rehabilitation, but not with antidepressants or just psychotherapy.

The first memory I have of an extreme reaction to a drug was when I had recently returned home from the hospital, when I was still resting because of the fractures. I started to appear very anxious and irritable. It didn't last long, but it was intense. Luckily, I was visited by a friend who is a doctor who normally works with drug addicts, helping them through their detoxification process. He could tell from my symptoms that I was clearly going "cold turkey" due to the removal of a small morphine patch I had been prescribed for the pain from the scar in my skull. I will never be able to thank him enough. Of course, the morphine withdrawal symptoms lasted another four or five unforgettable days, but knowing what was happening to me was a relief for everyone. I couldn't figure out why I was crabby and rude to everyone, and I couldn't stand myself either. I was told that this syndrome sometimes occurs in other people, but the surprise for the doctors was my extreme and unexpected reaction given the small quantity of morphine they had administered to me.

Here I would like to thank the doctors who were able to detect this hypersensitivity and immediately withdrew the medicine that they had originally prescribed, encouraging me to continue my neurological rehabilitation and to work through the emotional problems with psychotherapy.

> *TBI affects the brain in many ways, but the frontal and temporal areas are most commonly affected. This results in an alteration in the regulation of some neurotransmitters. These could be the reasons why a patient with TBI is more susceptible to certain drugs. Anticonvulsants, antidepressants and benzodiazepines may require*

fewer doses than usual to be effective or have more side effects, which calls for more rigorous monitoring of these drugs and their possible interactions with other drugs used.

Asymmetry

A few years into this, I am increasingly aware of the asymmetry that exists in my body, and that the body, which functions as a system, needs balance, or homeostasis as they say in systemic psychology, and to work in a balanced way.

Due to my accident, I have slight loss of hearing in one ear and vision in one eye, and there is considerable asymmetry between the healthy eye and ear and the injured ones. After a while, I understood that the problem of asymmetry is not due to the damage to the external function, by which I mean it does not simply manifest as a loss of diopters (units of optical power) or decibels. The problem is the difficulty with processing auditory and visual information that is not synchronised, because it is received by two receptors in different states. At one of my assessments at the neuro-functional rehabilitation centre, I understood this thanks to an exercise that was a revelation for me. The exercise consisted of reading a page with just my healthy eye, then reading the same page with just the injured eye, and then reading it again with both eyes together: I could see an unbelievable difference in speed, which was related to this lack of synchronisation.

The sensory difficulties in brain injury have a mixed component: the fact that they affect one specific organ (ear, eye, etc.) and that they alter the way the information we receive through these organs is processed in the CNS.

My good side constantly makes a huge effort to balance and compensate for the damage in my eyes, ears, etc., and this is very tiring. There is constant exertion from the eyes' accommodation and convergence reflex. As such, my healthy eye tries to adapt and make up for the damaged one, making a great effort because it can't bring itself in line; it tries to do the job of both the good and bad eyes, and something similar happens with my ears. I used to feel overwhelmed when, for example, I heard an ambulance, and I really couldn't tell which side it was coming from. My sons are a big help and they let me know immediately. When I mentioned this to one of the professionals who treated me, she explained that my good ear was trying to compensate for the other and, in some way, to hear what the other ear couldn't hear, which is why I wasn't able to tell properly where the sound was coming from.

> *A characteristic feature of unilateral hearing loss is the loss of "stereo", which manifests as difficulty locating the origin of auditory stimulus.*

Sometimes I consider agreeing to the surgery they have suggested to regain some of my hearing, not really to compensate for the loss of function – to which I have adapted – but to compensate for the "asymmetry fatigue". However, the idea of hearing more also scares me because of my hyperacousis.

Over the years, I have also discovered that I can tolerate sounds in stereo, which reach me through both ears at once, but not "mono" sounds, which reach me though just one ear. I have to limit the length of time I spend on the telephone, particularly on a mobile, which affects me more. I always listen with my right ear, because that is my healthy ear, but if I do so for too long, my head starts to hurt on that side, and then I feel dazed and listless.

Although it has been difficult to accept, I also now know that I should not use audio guides in museums. At first, I thought that this device would be good for me, as it could compensate for my distraction and would help me to concentrate on one artwork and then the next, and make the exhibition more enjoyable. I can still remember the mental exhaustion, stupor, general sickness and headaches after a long visit to an exhibition at Madrid's Thyssen-Bornemisza Museum with an audio guide. At the end of the visit, I felt an internal pain on the right side of my head that went behind my eye. The first few times this happened, I linked it to general fatigue but, after a number of similar experiences, I refined my assessment and realised that it had to do with auditory stimuli that come only from the right-hand side.

I normally try to avoid headphones in general, even though I'm listening through them in stereo, because after a while I feel like they cause auditory overstimulation. At home, I prefer to listen to music from a distance, sitting in an armchair.

My work now consists of trying to integrate this asymmetry into life, but it isn't always easy. I struggle to understand the contradictions within me. There are some conflicts I would like to investigate a little further, and to keep learning how to live with them: loss of sensitivity and hyperesthesia; hearing loss and hyperacousis; lack of awareness and over-analysis; and blocking or impulsivity when making decisions.

Auditory and optical hypersensitivity, diplopia, hyposalivation

After a few years, I found out that I have hyperacousis. I have lost some of the hearing in one ear due to the impact, but strangely, I also hear some sounds amplified. It would have been so useful to know about my extra sensitivity to noise from the beginning. It would have helped me in situations that neither I nor my family could understand, because nobody knew about this symptom.

I felt terrible after I had been in hospital for a long time, without being able to look after my children, and the first times I was with them I couldn't stand it if they screamed or made much noise – which is perfectly normal for children that age – and I didn't know why. I got anxious, I told them off, and I wanted to leave the room. Afterwards, I felt guilty, berating myself for being a "bad mother", and I was very anxious about this difficulty.

Understanding what was going on, thanks to professionals specialising in brain injury, albeit much later than I needed it, meant that I could accept what was happening and seek out tools to help me adapt to various situations. I always carry foam earplugs in my bag and I have others in my bedside table, to stop any noises making my sleep problems worse. Previously, I would avoid going to large supermarkets, children's birthday parties, the circus, etc. The good thing about knowing what it is is that now, although excessive noise still bothers me, I use earplugs or I look for a quiet spot to take the children and have a nice time. When I visit my parents or my in-laws, the earplugs always save me from the amplified noise of cutlery being taken out of the dishwasher, which I find unbearable and is something that saturates my "hard drive".

I am very shocked and scared by loud noises. Now that I know, I can try to prevent it. For example, my children know that if I'm driving and they want to open or close the windows in the back, which are folding and make a loud noise, they have to warn me, so I can anticipate it. When someone opens a can of Coca-Cola near my ear, or slams the car door when they get out, I really feel like I've been hit in the brain with a baseball bat. Once when I made that comparison, my son Álvaro told me I was exaggerating, but it's very real. The vibration from the "virtual blow" lasts a long time and takes a while to stabilise. I could really identify with Carole L. Starr, who explains in her book *To Root and To Rise: Accepting Brain Injury* that, because of her excessive sensitivity to noise, when an aeroplane passes overhead, she ducks because the noise is so loud to her that the plane seems to be flying straight at her.

She also tells us that an unexpected loud noise, like an alarm, will make her scream, lose her balance and sometimes even fall over (Starr, 2017).

If I'm walking down the street and I see works where they are drilling the asphalt or the pavement, I try to get away as quickly as possible, because of the experience I've had of having to pass by on other occasions. At first I felt embarrassed, but now I don't hesitate to stick my fingers in my ears when I walk past sites like that, if I can't avoid them altogether. Very loud music, the thuds of a basketball, plates crashing against each other in the sink . . . there are so many everyday noises that I would love to make disappear! But I know that blocking my ears is not the answer; it's better to learn to live with them.

On rainy days, when I've had to cancel outdoor plans with my children, I have managed to divide the house into different zones: one for playing and one for studying (both with the doors closed), the kitchen and a communal conversation area. At first, I thought that it wasn't my style to have the house compartmentalised, but now I'm happy with it. The distant noise of my son's ball banging in the hallway with the doors closed is much more bearable now, and I don't get angry with him for playing. If, in spite of everything, it still bothers me too much, I put in the earplugs and everything is much easier. It's amazing how such a cheap and simple tool has changed my life. I know that it would have spared me a lot of anguish and frustration to have known about the dizziness and hyperacousis earlier, so I would be very happy if this book can help someone else who is suffering from this without realising until they read about it.

Knowing my sensitivity, the way I jump at noises and my problems with concentrating, I have always chosen calm, discreet and very quiet people to help me with my domestic tasks.

> *With brain damage, we can see effects on hearing such as tinnitus or hyperacousis, which may occur together or present in isolation, although they are not frequent. In hyperacousis what happens is that, after the injury, the brain uses an abnormal route to conduct the stimulus, which is perceived as excessive. The therapeutic approach sometimes involves using stimulators that mask the sound (when there is also tinnitus) or behavioural therapy to modify the threshold of sound perception.*

Another effect I have noticed from the beginning, and which has been improving, is the dry mouth that my neurologists also related to the injury. I secrete less saliva, which means I have to keep drinking water constantly, because the dry mouth can even stop me from speaking. At first, this was a serious problem and I always had to keep water nearby and drink continually, as it could even cut me off mid-sentence if I didn't drink. Now I am much better and I tend to carry a bottle of water with me, although I don't need to drink as often. This hyposalivation increases much more if I'm nervous. For example, if I have to speak in a group for any reason, this effect increases considerably.

With visual information, I also need to make sure that it is not too intense, because my eyes do not adapt easily to change. When I move from a well-lit place to one with less light, I can't see anything for a couple of minutes, until I get used to it little by little. I have a particular sensitivity to light; I need total darkness to sleep, and I wake up very early if the tiniest bit of light gets in in the morning. When I travel abroad, I take an eye mask, because many countries don't use shutters and it's impossible to achieve absolute darkness. I normally wear sunglasses because of my sensitivity to excess light, and my damaged eye is my compass for knowing when I can handle stimulus in general. If I see that it is closing, this is a sign that I have to stop, that there is already too much stimulus. This sometimes happens when I don't take care to rest and I don't want to miss anything, if I keep watching a film until it's very late or I am reading an intense novel. My children are very wise when it comes to this and they always let me know, "Mum, your eye's closing, you must be worn out".

Diplopia, or double vision, caused by an injury to one of my cranial nerves as a result of the TBI, was another major consequence I had to learn to live with. The help of tools like my prism glasses has really improved things day-to-day, preventing my compensatory stiff neck and the constant sense of asymmetry. I've met many affected people who have the same physical symptom. I love Cristopher Yeoh's attitude, using this residual disability as the subtitle of his book, giving his deficit a fun and human meaning: *A Titled Point of View* (Yeoh, 2018). In this book, he recounts how, to face this impairment, he has had to learn to think consciously about other people's perspectives, because he lacks spatial awareness and perceives the world as flat or steep.

Part 4

Long-term adjustment and conclusions

Chapter 10

Identity reconstruction

Aurora Lassaletta and Christian Salas

Long-term emotional adjustment following an ABI

Adapting to changes following an ABI and accepting them in the long term are the rehabilitation targets I have been working towards for over fourteen years. I believe that, for the process to be successful, continued professional emotional support at all stages of neurorehabilitation is essential. Looking back, I can see how good it would have been for me and my family to have had that from the beginning. In Spain, as in many other developed and developing countries, this doesn't happen, as state funding for ABI rehabilitation is low. I would love for the model we aspire to in my country to be that of some of the rehabilitation centres in the UK, where they give long-term attention to the individual and to the family after an ABI (Skippon, 2013).

From experience, I know that the process of acceptance after such a sudden life change is not quick or easy. On the other hand, I have learned that this process stays with us for a long time; it never stops but slowly consolidates over the years. The extent to which we accept changes is closely related to our awareness of our deficits. These two elements, alongside the internalisation of tools and strategies that help with day-to-day functioning, are essential both to optimum identity reconstruction and to enjoying a full and meaningful life after ABI.

Accepting the changes and losses caused by brain injury is a long and complicated process. Due to the many cognitive changes, it is common for people not to understand exactly what has been lost or why a particular situation is painful or sad (Salas and Coetzer, 2015). The process of grieving for what has been lost usually requires greater awareness of the difficulties generated by the injury

> *and how they impact our daily life, our activities and our sense of who we are. Consequently, for many people affected, the process of accepting the changes can take many years, progressing slowly, hand in hand with increasing self-awareness and learning routines and compensatory strategies* (Klonoff, 2010).

I can now say that I've made considerable progress in accepting my new reality. I'm very aware of my losses, and I've recovered my sociability and good humour. My achievements have been supported by good planning of activities, always taking care to rest first, so that daily effort doesn't immediately result in a saturation of resources. Now I can laugh at myself and accept the repetition of my actions, or the limited variation in the things around me. For example, for the last five months, since I discovered a great recipe for *pisto* (a vegetable stew), I've cooked it at least three times a week, always the same meal, despite the raised eyebrows from my family. I've learned to live with this feeling of almost constant fatigue, without beating myself up. And I have found tools, like mindfulness or music, that have got me smiling again. There are also some impairments that I still struggle to integrate, but less and less. This journey has been a new experience, one that has helped me learn to tolerate frustration even better than before the accident. As Carole J. Starr says in her book *To Root and To Rise*, acceptance doesn't change the reality or the challenges of the symptoms of ABI, but it does change our subjective experience of them (Starr, 2017). The process of accepting my ABI has been a very important lesson in maturity for me. Although I still have some traces of impulsivity and egocentrism resulting from the injury, if I look closely at my new identity, I see greater maturity when it comes to facing the world and a greater sensitivity towards people who have suffered drastic and painful changes in their lives. As Silvia Abascal says in her book, illness teaches us a big lesson in humility, assessment, improvement and awareness (Abascal, 2013).

At first, after a sudden brain injury, we are overwhelmed by uncertainty. We don't know how we are going to get better or make progress, where our physical, cognitive or emotional rehabilitation will reach a plateau. This is why I always tell the participants in my support groups about the importance of trying to accept the moment you are living in, especially since we don't know what kind of progress we will make later. It isn't easy learning to live with this uncertainty. For me, being able to accept each stage that I've experienced has helped me to set realistic short-term goals. Throughout this journey of reconstruction, I've discovered tools that have helped me to reduce anxiety and function better in my day-to-day life. To settle into my new identity, it was essential for me to embrace these tools until I felt like they were my own.

Awareness of deficits and integrating the new me

Following a brain injury, our identity changes. Of course, the more serious the resulting deficits are, the more disruptive they are – not only the most obvious physical deficits, but also the cognitive, emotional and behavioural deficits. An ABI entails such a sudden and fundamental change that, at first, it's very difficult to recognise yourself in the new person you have become. Accepting your new life situation and adapting to it is also extremely complicated, because following a brain injury people can't clearly detect what changes have occurred in them. What I mean by that is that the problem of being aware of our deficits is inseparable from the task of reconstructing our identity. How do you accept or adapt when you don't even know who you are?

> *A common account from people after a brain injury is the experience of a "new me" (Nochi, 1998). For many, the brain injury becomes a milestone that marks a before and after in their personal biography, something many people describe as a rebirth. However, the "new me" is initially a stranger to the person affected, and it takes time and work to get to know them. When the discrepancy between the old and the new me is significant, people can experience intense emotional suffering (Gracey, Evans and Malley, 2009). When the changes caused by the injury are not physical, but cognitive, the fact that the cognitive problems are invisible to others can make the acceptance process more difficult.*

Who was I? Who am I? These questions inevitably went round and round in my head in the years following the accident. Not so much at first, because I didn't have a very high level of awareness of my deficits, as happens to many people who suffer a brain injury. The same thing happened to Christopher Yeoh, who describes in his interesting book how hard it was for him to understand that he had changed after his ABI, and how he even refused to accept it when other people told him so (Yeoh, 2017). After I woke up from the coma, neither I nor my family were very aware of what was happening to me; we didn't even know I had a brain injury and that that would have consequences. A lot of the time, I thought I was living in a bad dream and the next day I was going to wake up as the person I was before. Why didn't I listen to my family when they pointed out my limitations? My husband was surprised to see me start a conversation and not finish it. My speech was full of unfinished ideas. Often I couldn't remember things we had agreed, for example boundaries we agreed to set for our children. Then, when I didn't set the boundary and he told me I had forgotten, I would deny that we'd ever talked about it before. Why couldn't I realise at first that it wasn't going to be easy to go back to work, when the evidence showed me that just doing any simple activity saturated my cognitive capacity and left me tired for the rest of the day? Why did I believe that in no time I would be back to being the "multitasking woman" I used to be?

Looking back, I realise that this wasn't just happening to me; there was a lack of awareness in my family, too, thinking that my symptoms were temporary. We all believed that after a while everything would go back to normal. We associated my convalescence with an illness like a complicated episode of the flu or a broken leg. We didn't realise that it was much more than that. And we really knew very little about the effects on the brain of such a hard and sudden blow to the head. Of course, we also needed time to adapt emotionally to what had happened.

With time, observations made by my loved ones helped to slowly spark my awareness of my new limitations. *Why does it take so long for you to tell me something and why do you have to go all round the houses. Can't you just get to the point? This didn't used to happen to you, you're like our great-grandma! It takes so long between you trying to get up and you actually getting up – it's not normal!* Later, I was the one who started to realise that some of the symptoms were long term, that this wasn't a temporary thing. Now, I – and my husband and children, who live with me all the time – know full well that most of my current cognitive, emotional and behavioural symptoms are permanent and will stay with me for the rest of my life.

Following a very difficult spring and summer after the accident, the uncertainty of "Who am I now?" started to arise in parallel with my higher level of awareness of the changes in myself. This came at the moment my real impairments started to present themselves, as I was trying to resume some day-to-day activities. There I started to be conscious that there was something cognitive about these symptoms – something invisible! The lack of mobility and my physical impairments were evident to everyone. When I came home, I was in a wheelchair and I needed help getting around, making food and taking showers. But I assumed that, from my wheelchair, I would be able to direct the activities in my everyday life, I thought that my mental capacity was intact. I was very surprised to find that I couldn't keep the house tidy, but I blamed it on my tiredness, and at first I linked it to my physical convalescence. What I found really frustrating was not being able to organise tasks for the person who was helping me with things I still couldn't do because of my limited mobility. I couldn't even organise my own schedule. And that was something totally new to me. In my case, that was the moment when I started to question my new identity. Who was I now? I didn't understand anything: intellectually, I was the same as before with some things, but not with others. What was happening to my mind? I think there is a confusion, socially, between intellectual disability and cognitive disability, which we should be making more visible. A person can keep their intellectual capacity, but lose their organisational or executive capacity.

> *The lack of awareness of a person's illness is not only explained by cognitive changes secondary to the injury, but also by the interaction of these changes with emotional and cultural factors. Emotionally, both the person with brain injury and their relatives tend to play down the impact of brain injury, focusing on rehabilitation as a process that will get them back to normal. Culturally the general public has very little awareness of what a brain injury is and what its consequences might be, particularly in terms of cognitive and behavioural deficits.*

Four years after my accident I made this poster with words and drawings representing my condition and how I felt about my identity: "Who I was" and "Who I am". At that time I felt like there was an extreme division between these two aspects, something that was reflected by a strict and unmoveable line. Years later, I have realised that the line is much more broken, and there are shared aspects that I haven't lost, that I'm still recovering parts of my old identity, as well as discovering and creating new aspects of myself. The integration of my new identity, with old and new elements, has been and is still a difficult but wonderful task. Now I'm not as angry with the world because I need routines and am less adaptable than before, and I don't have dreams that after I take a nap I will wake up as the old Aurora, "ready for anything". There's nothing wrong with needing a little sleep after lunch. I can see it has its advantages. It helps me perform much better in the afternoon! I've learned a lot about the tools I need to enjoy life more. My family have learned them too. And I know that now I can help other people with ABI by sharing these tools with my groups, or encouraging them all to create their own "a la carte" tools, adapted to their own situations.

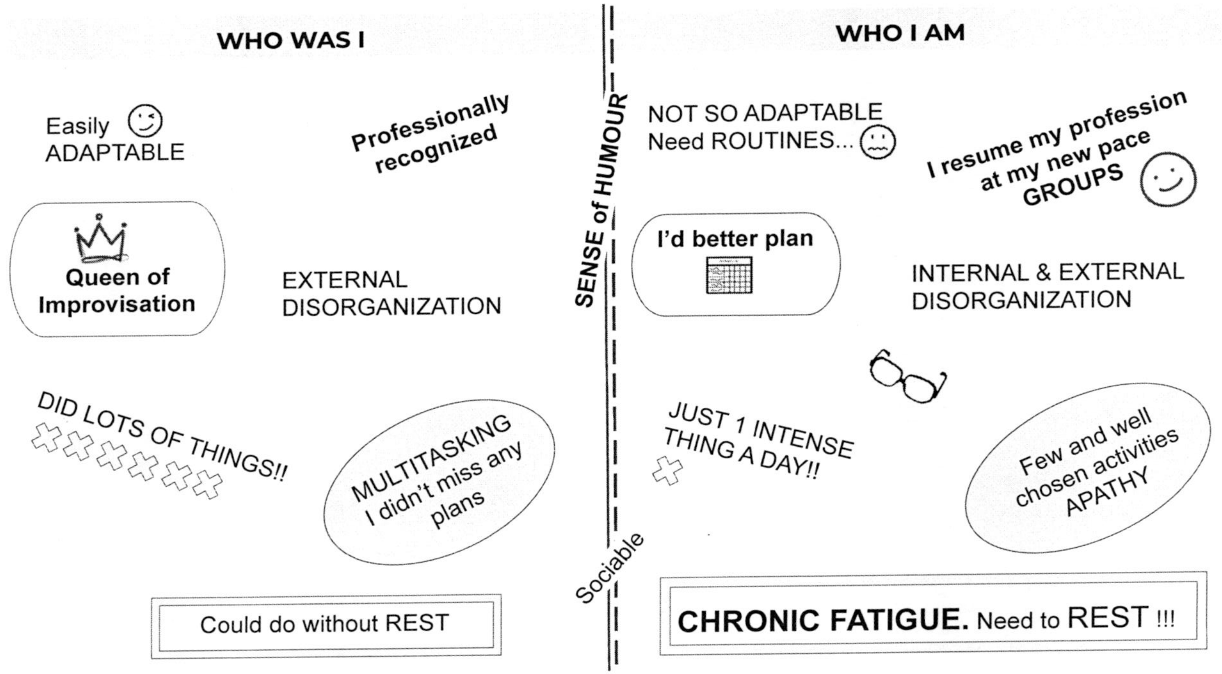

Figure 10.1 Identity map. The figure shows a description of self attributes before and after the injury.

Suddenly, I also realise that the passage of time works in my favour. I'm not as young as I was when I had the accident and I had to face all my residual disabilities. The advantage of not being so young anymore is that my friends, and the people around me, aren't either, and they've also started to get tired more easily than they used to. These days, I'm not surrounded by super active people who can "handle anything" and wouldn't dream of cancelling their plans, so I don't feel quite as different from everyone else as I used to. I never thought I would be happy about getting older. Every cloud has a silver lining!

For years I kept questioning my identity and now I've started to make peace with my new self. I feel like I've managed to integrate aspects that I've retained of my old identity with the recent additions, so that they form a new identity that represents who I am now. For me, one of the keys to this reconciliation was about recovering my identity as a woman, a partner, a mother and a friend. It was also essential to recover part of my professional identity, something that I really did miss. It's true that I've only been able to recover these identities in small doses and with new realistic targets adapted to my new situation. I am a woman, a partner, a mother, a friend and a clinical psychologist again, although sometimes I don't feel the same as I did before. At first, I felt like I didn't belong to any of these identities. Now I do feel like I belong. I had to find my ways of adapting to the roles that these new identities play, with the problems that go along with that – both I and my family had to accept that. But now I know who I am, I don't have that uncertainty anymore. I'm living much more happily with the new Aurora.

Feeling useful again has been central to reconstructing my identity. I feel recognised professionally, but in a different way. My professional activity consists of talks and clinical sessions I am specifically invited to give to inform people about invisible brain injury and, above all, emotional support for people with ABI in the "acceptance and adapting to change" workshops. The time I spend hosting those groups are my favourite moments of the week. What's more, the feedback I get from the participants in the group is very special. They say that the group couldn't be led by anyone else, because I'm a good professional, but also because I've also experienced the things we're talking about, and that's unique for them and helps them to listen to me. Although the group only takes up one and a half hours each week, the motivation, preparation, feedback and evaluation for it also take up some space. There is one way in which my identity now is starting to resemble my identity from before, and that is getting back into my professional space, a space for relationships where I help people as a psychotherapist. Of course the pace is different, and I can dedicate fewer hours; however, the internal enthusiasm and dedication to my work has only intensified. Before the accident, coordinating groups was also what I liked most about clinical psychology. Now, in addition, I feel that I'm part of a meeting with a peer group. I think that frequent meetings with people who have been through similar circumstances helps to reconstruct personality, and it gives us points of reference after we've lost some of our own. We feel like we belong to this group, when perhaps we don't feel like we belong to our professional group or our group of friends.

> *Identity reconstruction refers to the process by which, following a brain injury, people manage to integrate, or establish a coexistence between, aspects of their old and new self. The word "coexist" points to the fact that people, depending on the circumstances and context, fluctuate between their old and new selves. Identity reconstruction is closely linked to the ability to resume, or find, gradually, meaningful activities and roles – in other words, rediscovering a place in the world where it is possible to be productive, to love and to have fun.*

It is also an honour for me to feel that I now represent a group of people who have invisible symptoms. I get messages from all over Spain and Latin America telling me how beneficial it has been for ABI survivors and their families to read my book and my blog (www.danocerebralinvisible.com). Many people ask me for advice and I'm happy to help them raise awareness of their deficits. I realise that I have become a role model for some people and I'm very happy that the book or the blog can work like that and make me feel useful in that sense. My work is making these symptoms visible for those affected and for the people around them. It has a dual function, as raising awareness of the deficits helps with identity reconstruction and educates professionals so that they can facilitate this process. Some say that reading their patients' stories transforms professionals; it confronts them and helps them to see the overall nature of the treatment (Charon, 2012). My professional identity is now built on the integration of some of the clinical psychologist's tools I have recovered and the transmission of my own experience as an ABI survivor. After feeling very insecure as a professional for many years, I now really believe in what I'm saying, because I've lived it, and because people tell me that it helps them. I really recognise myself in this professional identity as someone who has lived through the experience and now supports others.

In the workshops, I stress the importance of feeling useful again after an ABI. For everyone in their own time, within their own possibilities and means. It can be anything from helping to whisk some eggs for cooking, folding socks or organising files on a computer to doing any kind of volunteering or getting back to work part time or even full time. For me, volunteering is a great way to give something of myself in short bursts. I highly recommend it for anyone who is not ready to go back to work, or has their doubts. It's a way to get yourself *almost* working.

In my years of experience with the groups, I've realised that reconstructing your own identity is very closely linked to gaining or increasing awareness of your deficits. A lack of awareness impedes the reconstruction and acceptance of our new identity. This is why I think it's very important for those affected, and their relatives, to understand ABI, and its most common symptoms and side effects. The information can really help to recognise new limitations that we didn't used to understand or associate with our brain injury. This information increases our own awareness of our new identity. We are often unaware of the changes that occur in us.

In the support groups we start to acknowledge symptoms in ourselves that we haven't been accepting. Although we don't all share exactly the same residual disabilities, we feel united because we've lived with and are working towards accepting our changes. In this space we feel understood. Some people become friends. There are professionals who offer to set up groups with people at different stages of recovery and with different levels of awareness (Muñoz Céspedes and Tirapu, 2001), because this helps to increase awareness of our limitations. By seeing deficits in other people, we learn about our own. As we learn more about ourselves and find out what resources we have now, and what losses we have suffered, we can begin to recognise ourselves in this new person we see in the mirror and continue with the work of adapting to the changes.

And it's not just us. Our loved ones will need to do this, too. An ABI affects everything around a person. An ABI in a parent, for example, can change the family immensely (Newby, Coetzer, Daisley and Weatherhead, 2013). I wish I'd had advice from the beginning to help me take on my new identity as a mother! Parenting is affected in many cases and help is needed from psychotherapists specialising in ABI, who can give support, teach ways to compensate for deficits and be points of reference at the most stressful moments of family life, such as your children's teenage years. This is why I believe meetings between relatives of people with ABI are very important. Often attention is focused exclusively on the affected person, while their whole family system suffers.

Emotional support for relatives given by professionals specialising in ABI is essential for the affected person's best possible recovery. (Evans-Roberts, Weatherhead and Vaughan, 2014). I can't feel good if I see that my family has had to adapt and change all their routines because of me, and on top of that they're suffering, as Christopher Yeoh explains in his book (Yeoh, 2018).

A short while ago, I went to the presentation of a book about videotherapy. I heard the psychologist who had written it talking about her work on self-image, strategies that can be carried out through mobile phones and cameras, and about the benefits this way of working can have on our relationship with our image, which is built of external and internal messages beginning in childhood (Rueda, 2018). I realised that, while our relationship with our own image is complicated for everyone, the difficulty people with ABI experience when coming to terms with their sudden new image is much greater. I also thought about how this kind of work can help us, very slowly and delicately, to tolerate, respect and even come to love our new identity. For example, it's taking me a long time to get used to my image with the asymmetry in my eyes and my face never looking expressive or animated. Looking at myself in the mirror, I see someone older than I feel inside. Yet, at the same time, when people say that I make them feel calm, I'm pleased to see that I've achieved enough inner calm and acceptance to be able to transmit it to other people. And, while I would like to radiate more vitality and agility, my current image does no more than reflect my current reality, by which I mean that it is a very real image of the new me, a bit asymmetrical, but at peace, more at peace with herself. I like the recommendation Christopher Yeoh gives in his post-ABI journal of taking care of the image of your new self, how you dress and present yourself to society (Yeoh, 2018).

After a long period of autotherapy, I've had to accept that I cannot resolve or manage some of the cognitive and emotional side effects on my own, and I have sought the advice of a neuropsychologist and psychotherapist, who helps me to deal with this aspect of my new identity. In these aspects I didn't even recognise myself in the person I was seeing. I never used to be the person I am now, with emotional ups and downs, unable to make decisions, unable to react immediately (for example, if I bump into someone in the street walking through a narrow space, or if I have to stop a fight between my kids or find the right words to set boundaries for a teenage son). These are the impairments I struggle to live with now, especially because I still don't have enough strategies to overcome them. I think it is very important to work with emotional and behavioural symptoms as well as the cognitive ones during neurorehabilitation. I haven't seen this in the rehabilitation programs offered around me. Luckily now, thanks to advances in medical care, there is an increasing survival rate for people with ABIs. From experience, I can see that many of the physical symptoms remain, but also the cognitive, behavioural and emotional symptoms. Treating these is essential, because they last for years and their treatment can improve quality of life for the person affected and for their family.

> *For a long time it was thought that people with ABI were not candidates for psychological support due to their cognitive difficulties. These days, the consensus is that psychological support in different forms (individual, family, group or couples psychological therapy) is a fundamental pillar of rehabilitation, especially in the long term. In general, psychological support is vital because it facilitates understanding and learning about the consequences of brain injury, offers a space to address social difficulties that emerge from the changes and facilitates the reconstruction of meaning (Balchin, Coetzer, Salas and Webster, 2017).*

There are some impairments that I just can't get along with. Something I still don't like is always being so tired. That is also the thing that makes the least sense to people around me. My children hate it because it often means that their plans outside the house get cut short, because I need to go home quickly and rest. This situation has improved now that my sons are teenagers, because they're starting to travel around by themselves on the metro or bus, and that makes things easier for all of us. They can extend their plans, and I can go home when I need to without feeling guilty. I am well aware that after a very intense event I will have to rest for a day or two afterwards. I really understand Allan Little's description of her wife Sheena McDonald sleeping for three days after presenting an important music award event, as a journalist, after her injury (McDonald, Little and Robinson, 2019).

Internalising compensatory tools

Internalising tools has been a very important process in my long-term development, and in the reconstruction of my identity. One of my main lessons from recent years has been the realisation that the feeling that I am getting better has nothing to do with a reduction in the ABI, or the recovery of functions, but rather the systematic use of tools that help me to cope with day-to-day problems.

> *The internalisation of tools and compensatory routines is a fundamental rehabilitation process, which can be considered an indicator of success. Compensatory tools (e.g. lists, calendars, alarms) allow us to hit targets (e.g. going to a meeting), bypassing the deficit (e.g. the memory problem). Compensatory routines (e.g. planning out the day and rationing amounts of energy) allow us to optimise limited cognitive resources, which increases our potential for being successful and feeling efficient. Usually after ABI, people reject strategies or routines because they are a reminder that they can't do things the way they used to. Then it's common to observe ambivalence in relation to using tools (e.g. they are helpful, but I prefer not to use them). Finally, in some cases, especially after repeated and systematic use, tools and routines become automatic and are experienced as part of the self. At this point, people say that they couldn't live without them.*

I have found my new "place in the world" and I want to consolidate it. Loving my new identity means accepting that I need my tools, my "cognitive crutches", and physical and emotional crutches, to contend successfully with family, social, professional and personal demands. I need them to achieve my goals, to be who I want to be. After all these years, I have become an expert in using my tools, and thanks to them I can adapt better to many demanding situations. These tools, which initially felt so strange, have almost become part of me, almost become internalised. I feel like my new identity is that of a manager: always being very conscious of how much I can do, planning according to the saturation of resources, knowing that if I overdo it there will be consequences. I recognise myself in the image of an "Administrator Aurora", with a bag full of tools to choose from according to what I need at the time. There are physical tools, but also cognitive ones.

When it comes to physical tools, I now know that thanks to my customised earplugs I can take a nap anywhere I go and get the rest I need. I've spent almost fourteen years trying to adapt to noise, but my hyperacusis has been there since the beginning. Although it has improved, just a little, it hasn't adjusted to my reality, which means I've had to find external tools like customised earplugs. I discovered them this year, and they have changed my life! They help me to get real sleep, not the light, interrupted sleep I had had to get used to because of the hyperacusis. Now I wake up every day and wonder how I didn't incorporate this tool much earlier. I hadn't done it because the doctors were telling me that I would eventually get used to the sounds, but it didn't turn out like that. Fourteen years is more than long enough for a confirmation.

I have so taken to my tools that, if I'm suddenly without them, I feel like a part of me is missing. One day, after countless searches, I couldn't find my glasses before I left the house for an all-day activity. Having to spend a full day without them was a real step backwards for me. Without my prism glasses I went back to seeing the world in duplicate again because of my diplopia. That day was hard, like going back in time. Because of that, when Christmas came, and knowing that I needed an eye test and therefore new lenses, I decided to ask for new glasses as a Christmas present, taking advantage of a two-for-one offer. It's incredible how much peace of mind I get from knowing that the desperate last-minute search for my glasses is so much easier now that I have two pairs. For the earplugs, I found a big, bright case that helps me locate them. I've bought duplicates of several things that I lose on a regular basis to reduce the everyday anxiety of not finding them. You might think I should just pay more attention to where I leave my glasses, keys, earplugs and everything else, and that would make it easier to find them. However, part of my new identity is responsible for maintaining a constant autofocus – this is exhausting and means that often, when I get home late, that intense self-observation has already dissolved in the elevator, and as soon as I walk into the house, I give it a holiday.

> *One important aspect of long-term acceptance is establishing a caring relationship with the "new me", particularly in relation to its difficulties. It has been noted that after a brain injury people can become hypervigilant and hypercritical of themselves regarding their deficits, generating negative emotions towards themselves and reducing their sense of effectiveness (Ashworth, Gracey and Gilbert, 2011).*

When it comes to cognitive tools, executive strategies have been very important. I've become so used to using them that it's hard to think of them as something outside of myself. And sometimes that can play tricks on me. Last year, I had a phase of maximum motivation, attributing the achievement of many of my new goals to an improvement in my symptoms or a reduction in my ABI. I even started to think, in a moment of euphoria, that my impairments were just anecdotal, and that maybe I could consider getting back into a routine and a job more like the one I had before the ABI thanks to this improvement. This enthusiasm came about because May 2018 was a very active month for me, when I went back to feeling more like the professional I used to be and when I took on many activities that I learned from and enjoyed very much. It was the first time in thirteen years that I had been to a professional conference outside Madrid. At the conference I felt that I could focus my attention much better during the majority of the papers, unlike years ago, and that my mind was working more quickly. Questions occurred to me as I was listening, and I managed to ask the speakers a few pertinent ones, even in English, at quiet moments during the breaks. I followed up the conference with a presentation of the book in the northern Spanish city of Pamplona; another presentation at the Official College of Psychologists in Madrid; and a paper at a Neurological Nursing Conference. At first, I only saw the facts. I was able to do these activities! I was pretty exhausted, but I had made a success of them. Inside, I felt like my old self again.

It didn't occur to me that, to do all these things, I had been using many of the tools that were now so normal for me, that had become internalised. I didn't notice that that month I had been more relaxed, as my younger child had been away (the older one is more independent and enjoys cooking) and I hadn't had to do so many "mum" tasks or household organisation as at other times. Nor did I realise that, although it seemed like the activities had turned out well spontaneously, I had spent a long time preparing them so that they would go as well as possible. I had scheduled each one in a different week, with a large gap between them, and I had taken care over the details so that my mind didn't suffer a saturation of resources. I didn't remember that, for activities in other cities, I'd found quiet accommodation, rather than staying with friends, to make sure I got the best possible rest and to be in the best possible state to face the demanding activities. At first, I thought that again I wasn't aware of my deficits, but then I realised that it was to do with a lack of awareness of the internalisation of the tools I had used to make things work. The tools had become automatic.

The following month, June, was a stressful month for me. We were all at home, plus a friend of my son's who was visiting from Ireland, and I kept up my sports, groups, meal planning and household organisation. I also think it was in June that all my fatigue from the previous month was expressed. I would get angry with myself and tell myself things like, "You can do it, you proved it in May! Why can't you do it now?" That month I went back to being all too conscious of my limitations. I couldn't even get any English words out when I was speaking to our houseguest. This time, I'd gone in on too many fronts; I felt like I couldn't even do the bare minimum and I was clearly suffering the consequences of saturation of resources.

However, in hindsight, I've realised that in general I have got better over the last fourteen years, much better, especially when it comes to attention. Having consulted with professionals, I am aware that the success of the activities in the month of May was not only due to a general overall improvement, but to the systematic use of the tools I have learned. Over the years, I have been incorporating tools that have become vital for me, without even knowing it. I have internalised them. Becoming aware of this has meant that now, instead of getting angry like I did in June because I felt like I hadn't really made that much of an improvement, I focus my energy on learning my new tools, knowing that by repeating them many times I will eventually internalise them, and they will become part of my new identity.

One recent lesson from my neuropsychological therapy has been the realisation that I have and will keep on having phases of all kinds, good phases and more difficult phases. This happens to everybody really, but perhaps I now experience the positive and negative charge of each phase more intensely, and I'm much more sensitive to the changes. Accepting that there will be different phases, and that improvement works like a pendulum, helps me not to get down and not to feel that a complicated phase is a complete disaster, or to get too excited about being back to my old self when a good phase comes around. In short, it's learning to live with the ups and downs and not fixing my identity to either extreme. I have also learned that these highs and lows will be less extreme if I can anticipate which tools I need to help prevent the feelings of frustration and failure, and to take each day as it comes.

One of the biggest lessons long-term has been learning to live with these pendular shifts without feeling like I'm going backwards. That has made the emotional ups and downs less intense, thanks to identifying them as symptoms and knowing that they're temporary. It's a nice theory, but then everyone has to come up with their own tools. Sometimes I've realised, after the fact, that I was wrong not to prepare a talk because I wanted to do it like the old Aurora: thinking that a short talk doesn't need preparation, or feeling like I had sufficient resources to come up with a good answer to questions on the fly. That strong feeling of going back to the person you were before is emotionally very powerful, and necessary. Without it getting out of hand, I think it's nice to feel like that again once in a while, to feel the same.

At first, I thought that, to construct my new identity, I would need to change the way I was and get a new personality that was much more structured, organised and disciplined than before. I tried and tried. Years of frustration and failure in this task made me aware of just how much effort I was devoting to changing myself into someone who is the complete opposite of the person I was. Finally, I stopped getting so stressed about it and decided to only make partial changes. I've never been very organised, or rather I've never needed much external structure to complete my tasks and hit my goals. Now I do need it, but I have a hard time sticking to strict schedules and timetables. It means I have to stop being me. "So what do I do?", I've asked myself many times. It has been very important for me to rediscover something that has always been a part of my personality – improvisation and the need to include changes and new things in my routine – but while being very much aware of the consequences this will have now. I no longer force myself to keep a schedule for meals and food shopping stuck to the fridge (which was a nightmare for me, because it felt like it belonged to someone else) and I'm happier this way, even though we do sometimes reach dinnertime and all I can think of, again, is the ham and cheese quiche we've already got coming out of our ears. Or I might not have any ingredients to improvise a last-minute dinner and I have to order something to be delivered. It's true that this balance between who I am and who I used to be does not resolve the day-to-day situation perfectly, but for my self-esteem it's vital to have recovered some elements of the old Aurora and, also, the hope that I will be able to find another tool that helps the new Aurora adapt better to current circumstances. I now have a list of possible meals on the fridge, as a "cognitive crutch" to stop me going blank when I need to think of options, and that way I can feel like I'm half improvising or I'm not always subject to a schedule. Paradoxically, a bit of structure is what gives me freedom!

> *One key element of identity reconstruction in the long term is being able to "salvage" aspects of the personality that were important to the person affected. This can refer to previous ways of relating to themselves, to others and to the world. The survival of these personality elements generates a smaller discrepancy between the old and the new self, facilitating an experience of "sameness" and "continuity". Through the use of strategies and routines, rehabilitation should help people to reconnect with these elements.*

My last summer holiday was the best in the last fourteen years. There is no doubt this had something to do with the anticipation and preparation of specific tools to compensate for my issues. On this holiday we were lucky enough to be invited to stay with friends at their house by the beach, in the south of Spain, together with other families we know. My excitement about the holiday was perfectly balanced by my fear that I wouldn't be able to survive and enjoy ten days of sharing a house, meals and organisation with fifteen people! The rooms were large family rooms, and I was immediately filled with fears of hyperacusis, needing a siesta and my particular difficulty with organising meals for so many people. But with time and foresight, and the inestimable help of the neuropsychologist, I was able to find a tool to alleviate each of my fears. This was when I got the customised earplugs, on the recommendation of one of the participants in my support groups, and they did their job brilliantly, letting me sleep or rest if I felt oversaturated by being surrounded by so many people. I was happy to read Cheryle Sullivan's recommendation for these sound filters prescribed by an audiologist, based on her own experience, in her practical book *Brain Injury Survival Kit*, full of simple and valuable tips and tricks (Sullivan, 2008). I also had time to prepare a list of possible meals I could make when it was my turn to cook, along with a shopping list and the selection for my team of kitchen assistants. I also thought about what would be the best times for me to cook without the stress of noise or people coming and going through the kitchen. To avoid distractions, burns and cuts, I chose the moments when everyone else had gone to the beach. What meals could I instruct my team to prepare that were easy for a large group and didn't require too much precision? Of course, all the teams had thought of spaghetti bolognese as their first option, but I had to think a bit harder. With time and patience I was able to plan several meals. Improvising them ad hoc would have been impossible, and it would have caused me a lot of anxiety. With all these tools and my "summer notebook" I was able to enjoy the holiday more than I have for years! Now I'll know how to handle other holidays in the future, whatever they might be. Being able to plan and use specific tools for each particular situation has been a vital lesson for me. After all these years, I've got so many tools in my bag than I can take my pick.

However, I do still have lots of things to work on, in the cognitive and emotional fields. I'm still contending with problems that make everyday tasks difficult. And adapting to life in a city like Madrid, where everything moves so quickly, and to the needs of my family, isn't always easy. What I miss most about my old identity is not being the "multitasking woman" I used to be, much like what happened to Cheryle Sullivan, who also suffered a significant brain injury (Sullivan, 2008). It's true that, if I'm careful with my rest and plan my activities well, there are moments where I can do several things at once, not as many as before, but more than a few years ago. I've started to be able to cook several dishes at once to save time. But the experience definitely leaves me too exhausted to do it regularly. As my awareness has increased, I've used new tactics such as turning off the music in the car when I'm driving. I'm even more conscious of how fragile my attention is, and how easily distraction can cause mistakes. So the happy image of me driving along singing my heart out to the music is reserved for very simple trips with no interference. I have also accepted that I'm slower now, and that my timing is different, as happens to many people affected (Roberts, 2014). Still today, when my children come back at me with the image of a bad-tempered mother who starts complaining about everything over breakfast, I find it hard to recognise myself in that new person, because I used to be much more calm and tolerant. I'm still recovering things and accepting that there are also aspects I can't recover. In all these years I haven't been able to adapt to noise while I sleep, but I have adapted to noise enough to go to a basketball game to watch my son play.

The personal and rehabilitation work never ends, which is why accepting that some deficits will never be resolved is so important. My experience with myself and with other ABI survivors, whom I have supported over the last ten years, has shown me that with strong emotional support everyone can take the process of acceptance in their own time and at their own speed, and these things have to be respected. As my acceptance grows, my relationship with my husband and children is getting better.

Chapter 11

Concluding remarks

Aurora Lassaletta

I would like this book, above all, to draw attention to the invisibility of some of the symptoms of ABI, especially the cognitive symptoms.

I would also like it to serve as a reflection, highlighting the need for early detection and rehabilitation for people who have ABI but show no clear physical symptoms.

There is no question that, in a very serious situation, the first thing a hospital must do is implement lifesaving measures. And I will be eternally grateful to all the doctors and healthcare staff whose work means I am still here today. They operated on me, helped me through the initial critical situation, did the tests and neurological assessments required for a serious head injury, treated my fractures and discharged me when I no longer needed hospital care.

The hospital's work is very apparent, but the next steps are not as clear. Life goes on after survival and, although it's not critical, it is very important for the person affected, when they are discharged, to know how to manage their subsequent recuperation, especially if there could be functional repercussions from the brain injury, including cognitive issues (Easton, Atkin and Dowell, 2006; Easton, 2016).

I would also like to stress the need for neuropsychologists in hospitals who can take charge of the initial assessment of patients admitted with TBI, strokes or other ABIs. This assessment is very important in planning treatment and rehabilitation goals when the patient is discharged. Another essential role of neuropsychologists is providing information to the patient's family about not only the physical but also the cognitive, behavioural and emotional symptoms that can appear as a result of brain injury, and encouraging them to seek neuropsychological treatment if they detect any of these symptoms.

I am convinced that early detection and management of slight and moderate ABI would be positive, and even profitable, steps for the healthcare system. This should be accompanied by good neurorehabilitation that, although costly in the short term, could mean major savings for the system long term (Prigatano and Pliskin, 2002; Wilson, Winegardner and Ashworth, 2014). Similarly, it would constitute huge progress for specialised professionals to work as a "one-stop shop" for medical decisions about the long-term treatment and rehabilitation of this group.

I am very grateful for the treatment I have received at CEADAC in Madrid. That is where I began my cognitive rehabilitation. CEADAC has just a few professionals to treat a large, and ever-growing, number of people with brain injury. It would really help to have more specialists and more public rehabilitation centres in other Spanish cities. But, most of all, providing these services would allow time for properly tailored treatment for each and every person, and subsequent monitoring and management to ensure that they make the best possible recovery.

I understand how difficult diagnosis is, especially if the ABI is mild, or if even the person themselves is unaware of what's happening to them. Some symptoms may take time to appear and require specific neuroimaging tests (Roberts, 2014). From my experience, I would ask health and social care professionals, when they meet a patient who has suffered a stroke, TBI or other brain pathologies (or any random hit to the head or neck, an unexpected collision with a football, a fall from a bicycle or scooter, whiplash from a car crash with impact from behind, etc.), to ensure that a serious assessment has been made of whether any brain injury has occurred before they start with the standard protocol and treatment. This applies even if the patient does not have very visible dysfunctional symptoms. I understand the high amount of pressure on professionals and the lack of time that they have to dedicate to patients, especially in the public health service. But, as Natalie, a patient, says in the book *Life after Brain Injury: Survivor Stories* (Wilson, Winegardner and Ashworth, 2014), people with ABI need to be listened to, however slow and confused we are when we explain our symptoms.

As clinical psychologists, we need to be more aware of the similarity between certain symptoms of subclinical depression and those caused by brain injury, to make a successful differential diagnosis. From my point of view, neuropsychological and psychotherapeutic work is essential and needs to be highly coordinated and integrated.

As Julio Agredano recommends in his book *Y después de un ictus, ¿qué?* (*What To Do After a Stroke?*), it takes work to get back to work (Agredano, 2015). Over the years, I have confirmed how important it is to think seriously about the possibility of people with ABI going back to work, where possible, with appropriate support and contact between company and rehabilitator for the best gradual and careful return. There are now a number of books written by people affected and by professionals that shed plenty of light on this issue (Denton, 2008; Easton, 2016; Wilson, Winegardner and Ashworth, 2014; Yeoh, 2018).

I have been helped so much by the people who always believed in my brain injury, or rather who believed me when I talked about the effects I was feeling. But I am aware that I was also helped by the people who never believed in it. I'm sure they awakened my rebellious side and my need to research and prove that there was a reason for the symptoms I was detecting and that they required specific treatment.

I was not aware of the benefits I would gain from my book's publication in Spain in 2017, and the warm reception and feedback from other people with ABI, and their families and healthcare professionals. The interest in the book from readers and publishing houses in other countries has made me even more sure of what I'm saying, as an ABI survivor and as a professional, after years of not believing in myself. It doesn't seem true that a few years ago I didn't want my name to appear as the author of this book and I was planning to use a pseudonym, because I was ashamed that people would read about my life and my personal story. I feel that taking the step of making myself visible as someone affected by ABI was important for me, and for other people in the same situation.

The book presentations, the blog I started to write when the book was published in Spain in May 2017 (www.danocerebralinvisible.com), the clinical sessions to which I was invited and the papers I gave at conferences represented significant progress for me in the structure of my message, the reconstruction of my professional and personal identity and my self-esteem. I learned a lot in that time and I want to keep learning a lot, eagerly, at my own pace. My intuition was crucial in the first few years, to get to the symptoms and possible treatments, and my self-therapy continues.

After a fourteen-year journey of learning and emotional training, I now know that my disability is just another of my features. My disability does not define me. And now I believe in my abilities.

References

Abascal, S. (2013). *Todo un viaje*. Barcelona: Temas de hoy.

Agredano, J. (2015). *Y después de un ictus ¿qué?* Madrid: San Pablo.

Ashworth, F., Gracey, F., and Gilbert, P. (2011). "Compassion Focused Therapy after Traumatic Brain Injury: Theoretical Foundations and a Case Illustration". *Brain Impairment*, 12(2), 128–139.

Baddeley, A. D., Kopelman, M. D. and Wilson, B. A. (2002). *The Handbook of Memory Disorders* (2nd ed.). Chichester, UK: John Wiley and Sons.

Balchin, R., Coetzer, R., Salas, C. and Webster, J. (2017). *Addressing Brain Injury in Under-Resourced Settings: A Practical Guide to Community-Centred Approaches*. London: Psychology Press.

Benedet, M. J. (2002). *Fundamento teórico y metodológico de la neuropsicología cognitiva*. Madrid: IMSERSO.

Bensoussan, L., Viton, J. L., Schieppati, M., Collado, H., Milhe de Bovis, V., Mesure S. and Delarque, A. (2007). "Change in Postural Control in Hemiplejic Patients After Stroke Performing a Dual Task". *Archives of Physical Medicine and Rehabilitation*, 88, 1009–1015.

Bilbao, A. and Díaz, J. L. (2008). *Guía de manejo cognitivo y conductual de personas con daño cerebral*. Madrid: IMSERSO.

Charon, R. (2012). "At the Membranes of Care: Stories in Narrative Medicine". *Academic Medicine*, 87(3), 342–347.

Christensen, A. L. and Uzzell, B. (1999). *International Handbook of Neuropsychological Rehabilitation*. New York: Plenum/Kluwer.

Denton, G. L. (2008). *Brainlash: Maximize Your Recovery from Mild Brain Injury* (3nd ed.). New York: Demos Health.

Doidge, N. (2007). *The Brain that Changes Itself: Stories of Personal Triumph from the Frontiers of Brain Science*. New York: Penguin Books.

Easton, A. (2016). *Life after Encephalitis: A Narrative Approach*. London: Routledge.

Easton, A. and Atkin, K. (2011). "Medicine and Patient Narratives". *Social Care and Neurodisability*, 2, 33–41.

Easton, A., Atkin, K. and Dowell, E. (2006). "Encephalitis, a Service Orphan: The Need for More Research and Access to Neuropsychology". *British Journal of Neuroscience Nursing*, 2, 488–492.

Evans-Roberts, C., Weatherhead, S. and Vaughan, F. (2014). "Working with Families Following Brain Injury". *Revista Chilena de Neuropsicología*, 9(1).

Goldstein, G. and Beers, S. R. (1998). *Rehabilitation of Brain Function*. New York: Plenum Press.

Gracey, F., Evans, J. J., and Malley, D. (2009). "Capturing Process and Outcome in Complex Rehabilitation Interventions: A 'Y-shaped' Model". *Neuropsychological Rehabilitation*, 19(6), 867–890.

Kapoor, N. and Ciuffreda, K. J. (2002). "Vision Disturbances Following Traumatic Brain Injury". *Current Treatment Options in Neurology*, 4, 271–280.

Klonoff, P. S. (2010). *Psychotherapy after Brain Injury: Principles and Techniques*. New York: Guilford Press.

McDonald, S., Little, A. and Robinson, G. (2019). *Rebuilding Life after Brain Injury*. Abingdon: Routledge.

Muñoz Céspedes, J. M. and Tirapu Ustárroz, J. (2001). *Rehabilitación neuropsicológica*. Madrid: Síntesis.

Newby, G., Coetzer, R., Daisley, A. and Weatherhead, S. (2013). *Practical Neuropsychological Rehabilitation in Acquired Brain Injury: A Guide for Working Clinicians*. London: Routledge.

Nochi, M. (1998). "'Loss of Self in the Narratives of People with Traumatic Brain Injuries: A Qualitative Analysis". *Social Science and Medicine*, 46(7), 869–878.

Osborn, C. L. (2000). *Over My Head: A Doctor's Own Story of Head Injury from the Inside Looking Out*. Kansas City: Andrews McMeel.

Pastor, P. (2019). *Los años del monzón*. Madrid: Libros.com.

Peydro de Moya, M. F., Baydal Bertomeu, J. M. and Vivas Broseta, M. J. (2005). "Evaluación and rehabilitación del equilibrio mediante posturografía". *Rehabilitación*, 39(6), 315–323.

Prigatano, G. P. (1999). *Principles of Neuropsychological Rehabilitation*. New York: Oxford University Press.

Prigatano, G. and Pliskin, N. H. (eds.) (2002). *Clinical Neuropsychology and Cost-Outcome Research: An Introduction*. Hove, UK: Psychology Press.

Roberts, J. (2014). *6 Steps to Understanding and Coping with Mild Traumatic Brain Injury: Strategies to Dealing with Cognitive Function Loss, Self Esteem, Relationships and Fatigue*. California: CreateSpace.

Rueda, O. (2018). *Videogestalt: Psicoterapia audiovisual*. Colección: Vídeo, educación y terapia. Madrid: Espaciointerno Ediciones.

Salas, C., Vaughan, F., Shanker, S. and Turnbull, O. (2013). "Stuck in a Moment: Concreteness and Psychotherapy After Brain Injury". *Neurodisability and Psychotherapy*, 1, 1–38.

Salas, C. E. and Coetzer, R. (2015). "Is Concreteness the Invisible Link Between Altered Emotional Processing, Impaired Awareness and Mourning Difficulties after Traumatic Brain Injury?" *Neuropsychoanalysis*, 17(1), 3–18.

Skippon, R. (2013). Supporting families and parenting after parental brain injury. In Newby, G., Coetzer, R., Daisley, A. and Weatherhead, S. (eds.) *Practical Neuropsychological Rehabilitation in Acquired Brain Injury: A Guide for Working Clinicians*. London: Routledge, pp. 295–320.

Sohlberg, M. M. and Mateer, C. A. (1989). *Introduction to Cognitive Rehabilitation: Theory and Practice*. New York: Guilford Press.

Starr, C. (2017). *To Root and To Rise: Accepting Brain Injury*. Cape Elizabeth: Spiral Path.

Stern, Y. (2007). *Cognitive Reserve: Theory and Applications*. New York: Psychology Press.

Sullivan, C. (2008). *Brain Injury Survival Kit: 365 Tips, Tools and Tricks to Deal with Cognitive Function Loss*. New York: Demos Medical.

Suter, P. S. and Harvey, L. H. (2011). *Vision Rehabilitation: Multidisciplinary Care of the Patient Following Brain Injury*. New York: Routledge.

Wilson, B. A. (1999). *Case Studies in Neuropsychological Rehabilitation*. Oxford: Oxford University Press.

Wilson, B. A. (ed.) (2003). *Neuropsychological Rehabilitation: Theory and Practice*. Lisse: Swets and Zeitlinger.

Wilson, B. A. (2009). *Memory Rehabilitation: Integrating Theory and Practice*. New York: Guilford Press.

Wilson, B. A., Dhamapurkar, S. and Rose, A. (2016). *Surviving Brain Injury After Assault: Gary's Story*. Hove, UK: Psychology Press.

Wilson, B. A., Evans J. J., Gracey, F. and Bateman, A. (2009). *Neuropsychological Rehabilitation: Theory, Models, Therapy and Outcomes*. Cambridge, UK: Cambridge University Press.

Wilson, B. A., Herbert, C. M. and Shiel, A. (2003). *Behavioural Approaches in Neuropsychological Rehabilitation: Optimising Rehabilitation Procedures*. Hove, UK: Psychology Press.

Wilson, B. A., Winegardner, J. and Ashworth, F. (2014). *Life after Brain Injury: Survivors' Stories*. Hove, UK: Psychology Press.

Winson, R., Wilson, B. A. and Bateman, A. (eds.) (2017). *The Brain Injury Rehabilitation Workbook*. New York: Guilford Press.

Yeoh, C. (2018). *A Different Perspective after Brain Injury: A Tilted Point of View*. London: Routledge.

Zuzuárregui, J. P., Bickart, K. and Kutscher, S. J. (2018). "A Review of Sleep Disturbances Following Traumatic Brain Injury". *Sleep Science and Practice*, 2:2.

Index